CATAMARAN SAILING

FROM START TO FINISH

Books by Phil Berman

Winning in Catamarans

Multihull Racing: The Hobie Cats (with Fred Miller)

Catamaran Racing: From Start to Finish

The Search for Meaning

The Courage of Conviction

The Ageless Spirit

The Journey Home

The Courage to Grow Old

CATAMARAN SAILING

FROM START TO FINISH

Phil Berman

Illustrations by Bradford Scott

W. W. Norton & Company
New York • London

For information about permission to reproduce selections from
this book, write to Permissions, W. W. Norton & Company, Inc.,
500 Fifth Avenue, New York, NY 10110

The text of this book is composed in Versailles
    with the display set in Helvetica Neue Extended
Book design and composition by Faith Hague Book Design
Manufacturing by Courier Westford

Library of Congress Cataloging-in-Publication Data

Berman, Phil
        Catamaran sailing : from start to finish / Phil Berman ;
    illustrations by Bradford Scott.
            p.   cm.
        Includes bibliographical references (p.).
        ISBN 0-393-31880-X (pbk.)
        1. Catamarans. I. Title.
    GV811.57.B466 1999
    797.1'24—dc21   98-54158
                                                     CIP

W. W. Norton & Company, Inc., 500 Fifth Avenue, New York, NY 10110
    http:// www.wwnorton.com
W. W. Norton & Company Ltd., 10 Coptic Street, London WC1A 1PU

    7 8 9 0

For Aaron

CONTENTS

INTRODUCTION TO THE REVISED EDITION

It all seems so long ago. The year was 1969, and the renegade surfer Hobie Alter had just introduced his latest invention, the Hobie Cat 14. I was standing on the dock of a stuffy yacht club in Newport Beach, California, when I watched Hobie himself demonstrate his quirky little cat. As I recall, everyone was talking about how very fast the boat was and how strange it was to see it "fly a hull." As for me, all I could think about was the large trampoline that spanned the two hulls. What a perfect spot to learn how to kiss a girl! Ah, to be thirteen again.

Well, I ended up buying one of those Hobie Cats and falling in love with sailing, along with a few girls. Little did I know that my love of catamaran sailing would eventually take me around the world. Even today, at the age of 42, I continue to sail a catamaran on the Great Lakes, my 41 footer, *Spectris*.

At the age of seventeen, in 1974, I wrote the first book on catamaran racing, *Multihull Racing the Hobie Cats*, which has now gone out of print. Today I remain an author, but have turned my attention to seemingly loftier matters, for the books I write focus on the perennial human hunger for a deeper sense of purpose in life. Now my books carry such titles as *The Search for Meaning*, *The Courage of Conviction* and *The Journey Home*. Still, of all the books I have written, this one may well have brought the most meaning to my readers' lives. In print now for more than fifteen years, *Catamaran Sailing: From Start to Finish* has introduced many thousands of people to this natural, non-polluting sport which puts them in touch with the enchanting world of wind and sea.

Over the past fifteen years since this book first appeared much has changed in the catamaran scene. Many boats have come and gone. New techniques have developed for sailing and racing catamarans. And new types of sails have been invented. Also, many of the names and numbers of catamaran companies and service organizations have changed. It is for these reasons that we decided to update this book, including an entire new chapter on performance sails, a new appendix with names and numbers of catamaran manufacturers and suppliers, and a wide range of new photographs that highlight the latest catamarans to come on the scene since this book was first published in 1982. I have also edited the entire text carefully to insure that the information provided here is current and accurate.

Today I find myself teaching my seven-year-old son how to sail my catamaran. His world is full of questions about the jib, the rig, how the wind blows over the water, which boat is faster than this boat and so on. More than anything, he seems to love just sitting on our cat, imbibing the harmony, the silence, the peace of water life. Through his eyes I see the world fresh again. It is a world of mystery, gratitude, joy, simplicity. I can't be a kid again (wouldn't want to be), but at least I can still remember what it was like to look upon the world with a boundless sense of openness, adventure, and hopefulness. As the late I.F. Stone once said, at the age of 88, "My aim is to die young, as old as possible." Certainly it is my hope that this book will contribute in some way to your own "growing young" process, no matter how "old" you may be. Sailing is, after all, a kind of grace, a kind of magic. It can fill you with joy—so long as you allow the wind to set you free.

HOW TO USE THIS BOOK

This is a complete course in catamaran sailing for the beginner, as well as the semi-experienced sailor who wants to become more skilled in the arts of tuning, handling and racing.

The teaching method used in this course is a cyclic one. In the first chapters you are presented information at a very basic level on a variety of subjects, and then brought back to these subjects in later pages at more advanced levels. This enables you to advance at the pace you like without your having to learn too much too soon, or more than you wish to learn at all. If you ever want to jump ahead, to look at something in greater detail, chapter reference numbers will follow important subjects in the text, and all subjects are listed with page reference numbers in the table of contents.

To get the most benefit from this book, read Part I before you go sailing. Part II is more advanced and its chapters will be difficult to grasp unless you have mastered the basics. Chapters eleven and twelve are the most complicated. They present a very concise introduction to catamaran race course thinking. These chapters will need to be read and re-read as you begin to race.

Every subject seems to have its special vocabulary, and sailing doesn't deny this rule. Although the text has been written with a simplified vocabulary, you will need to learn some sailing jargon. If a term appears, and its meaning is unclear, refer to the glossary at the back of the book.

Take your time, read carefully, and sail your cat in heavy air only after you are confident that you really know the ways of sail.

Good Luck.

PART I
LEARNING THE BASICS

1/
SHOPPING AROUND FOR A CAT

The catamaran is an exciting multi-purpose sailboat. Many cats reach speeds over 28 knots and can be sailed in almost all conditions, including riding in and out of surf. And cats are a good value. Compared to a high performance monohull of similar size, the majority of cats are inexpensive.

If you already own a cat or have a friend who does, you're in good shape for a lot of fun on the water. But if you don't have a way of getting out on a cat and are interested in buying one, do some thinking first. There are many things to consider. What you want is a cat that will fit your needs best, and finding it takes some investigating.

RACE OR DAYSAIL?

If you plan on puttering around, flying an occasional hull (lifting a hull out of the water), or picnicking on the trampoline, many cats will work well. The daysailor doesn't have to be "class conscious" unless the benefits of buying a certain class cat increase cruising enjoyment. Primary considerations for the daysailor include ease of rigging, ability to accommodate a few friends, and serviceability by a nearby dealer. While the cruiser may not need a strong class in his area since he won't be racing, it is a good idea to consider the more popular classes because a "known" class cat is much easier to sell.

Being class conscious is, however, all-important if you are interested in racing. The first thing to do is get an idea of what the overall racing picture is in your area. Dealers and local cat sailors are the people to talk to in this regard. They can put you in touch with local fleet officers and can tell you which fleets are the most active in the area.

Some classes such as Hobie, Prindle, and Nacra have excellent racing programs supported by their manufacturers. Smaller classes often don't have this kind of support, which leads to poor racing programs. Obviously, it's not wise to buy a cat that has a small class—it's no fun not having anyone to race against.

Also, consider how much sailing fast is important to you. If extra fast sailing is your primary concern, then an all around cat that would be best for daysailing and racing might not be what you want. All-out speed (but not necessarily good one-design racing) calls for a lightweight *symmetrical-hulled cat* rather than a more durable and versatile *asymmetrical-hulled* cat.

Figure 1

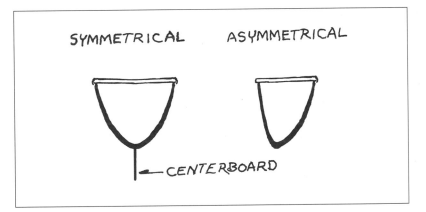

A symmetrical hull is fully round and is the fastest proven hydrodynamic hull shape (figure 1). Symmetrical-hulled cats have daggerboards or centerboards that improve upwind performance.

An asymmetrical cat is flat on one side of its hulls and curved on the other (figure 1). Asymmetrical cats don't need centerboards or daggerboards, which makes for much easier beach launching and surfing at the expense of a small loss in upwind performance and overall hull speed. However, the versatility of asymmetrical cats has made them the most popular

racers. So, a slightly faster cat certainly does not make for a better racing cat.

TO TRAILER OR NOT?

If you're one of the few lucky sailors who has access to a beach or a mooring, you don't have to be too concerned with ease of rigging or transportation.

But the majority of cat owners live away from the water and must use a trailer to get their cats to the beach or marina. An easily transported cat makes things much easier. Cats with a beam over eight feet must be trailered on a tilt trailer or dismantled each time they are moved. Cats like the Olympic Tornado are big and fast, but they do require extra rigging time for this reason. For someone considering such a cat, the pros of speed and racing must be weighed against the cons of extra hassle each time the boat is rigged and down rigged.

Weight is another consideration for the trailer sailor. Dragging a 400-pound cat across a beach will put hair on your chest for sure. And there may not always be willing hands around to help you and your cat to the water. Buying a set of beach wheels can be a big help here if you can't trailer your cat right down to the water's edge.

HOBIE WAVE	
LENGTH OVERALL	13'
BEAM	7'
WEIGHT	235 LBS.
MAST HEIGHT	23'
SAIL AREA	95 SQ. FT.

SHOPPING AROUND
FOR A CAT

Trailer sailors should also consider what it takes to rig certain cats. You will soon wish you had a smaller cat if stepping and unstepping the mast requires a lot of time and energy. Generally, larger cats have more complicated rigging and are the most difficult to transport. Ask your local dealer or cat sailors how easy it is to rig and downrig the boat you are considering. Better yet, watch or help someone rig one of the boats. If it seems to be a lot of hassle, keep looking for the right cat. (For more information on trailering see chapter 17.)

HOBIE 16
LENGTH OVERALL   16'7"
BEAM   7'11"
WEIGHT   320 LBS.
MAST HEIGHT   29'
SAIL AREA   218 SQ. FT.

A SOLO OR A DUO?

Do you think you might be sailing alone sometimes even though you haven't planned on it? Or, conversely, will you be

LEARNING THE BASICS

sailing with others even though you haven't planned on it? These are questions you should think about.

PRINDLE 16

LENGTH OVERALL	16'
BEAM	7'11"
WEIGHT	300 LBS.
MAST HEIGHT	26'
SAIL AREA	189 SQ. FT.

When you get a cat, you'll probably hear from just about everyone that they would love to go sailing sometime. Naturally you want to share the thrill of cat sailing, but you should ask yourself: "Now, are they really interested or are they just into giving it a try?" It can be pretty depressing when you want to go sailing and you discover that your sailing mate or mates have lost interest. So then it's either singlehanding or spending time looking for crew when you want to be on the water. And just the opposite can happen. After spending some time on the beach watching you cat around, would-be guests might end up overcrowding your small cat.

A WORD ABOUT COST

After deciding on the cat of your dreams, look into the cost. Most quality cats of similar size cost about the same, give or

SHOPPING AROUND
FOR A CAT

take a few hundred dollars. Beware of cats that cost considerably under the norm. When in doubt, go for a well-known cat that's priced in the middle of the market.

USED CATS

Many skippers new to sailing buy a used cat. Used cats are cheaper than new ones and often there isn't much difference in condition between them. But the novice buying a used cat has to know what to look for to avoid trouble. It's difficult to tell cosmetic problems from potentially costly structural problems. Dealers and other cat sailors can be a big help here since most of them know a good cat when they see one. Have someone knowledgeable look your used beauty over before you take on the pink slip. Used cats can often be bought from dealers and this isn't a bad way to go since dealers are responsible for servicing what they sell and they also have a reputation to protect.

A dealer or knowledgeable sailor can also help you determine the true value of any "extra gear" a used cat is being sold with. Some extra gear can really be worthwhile—while other extras may be of no value to you, or anyone else for that matter.

TIPS ON BUYING A USED CAT

If you know where to poke your nose, it's pretty easy to weed out a bad boat. You may be able to get a big, fast cat for seemingly little money, but that doesn't mean you got a good deal.

A competitive Tornado can cost up to $12,000 while a non-competitive Tornado (a dog) may sell for less than $1,500. The market value of a cat is determined by its popularity and ability to perform its function. A non-competitive Tornado is worthless to the racing sailor but might be ideal for someone who wants a big, fast, cruising cat. However, an outdated racing cat may be unseaworthy or too complicated for beginners.

"Oddball" cats can also be had at a "bargain." An oddball cat is usually no longer in production or was someone's back-yard project. Oddball cats are usually more trouble than they're worth—even if they cost next to nothing. Replacement parts are tough to find. And what happens if something major needs to be replaced? Oddballs are tough to sell, too—that's why you can get one dirt cheap.

INSPECT THE HULLS

Many summers of being dragged across the beach can really wear down a cat's hulls. So this should be the first thing you check when inspecting the hulls. Hulls that have been worn flat

HOBIE 17 SPORT	
LENGTH OVERALL	17'
BEAM	8'
WEIGHT	340 LBS.
MAST HEIGHT	29'9"
SAIL AREA	200 SQ. FT.

will need reglassing—which is a major project. Also look for any fractures in the fiberglass or delamination of the glass from the foam (in foam sandwich constructed cats).

Loose *pylons* (the metal posts that rise from Hobie 14 and 16 hulls to the trampoline frame) are another source of problems. Fractures in the gel coat are easy to spot. And, while delamination is often impossible to see, it can be detected by pressing on the hulls and decks. If some areas collapse to the touch or are noticeably softer than others, delamination may exist—which can lead to an unsafe boat.

Also check the seams where the hull is sealed to the deck or where the two hull halves are sealed together. If cracking appears or the seam is questionable, sharpen your investigation. Look for irregular color spots in the finish. If one area is brighter than the other, it may mean that the boat had a physical confrontation with Captain Nemo and the *Nautilus* or something. There's nothing wrong with a boat that has been repaired well, except for possible added weight and a lower resale value.

HOBIE 18SX
LENGTH OVERALL   18'
BEAM   8'
WEIGHT   400
MAST HEIGHT   31'9"
SAIL AREA   240 SQ. FT.

LEARNING THE BASICS

RUDDERS AND BOARDS

Both rudders and daggerboards must be straight. Warped rudders or daggerboards will have to be replaced. Chipped boards can be patched. Look closely at the entire rudder assembly to see if the *gudgeons* (stainless steel brackets

HOBIE 20	
LENGTH OVERALL	19'6"
BEAM	8'6"
WEIGHT	420 LBS.
MAST HEIGHT	33'6"
SAIL AREA	250 SQ. FT.

SHOPPING AROUND
FOR A CAT

NACRA 570

LENGTH OVERALL	18'6"
BEAM	8'2.5"
WEIGHT	360 LBS.
MAST HEIGHT	29'9"
SAIL AREA	225 SQ. FT.

mounted to the transoms of the hulls) are secure. Have they been torn out and replaced after the boat made a kamikaze landing on some reef? Steer the cat on its trailer and see if it feels sloppy or not. If the assembly seems to wobble, new bushings may be needed. If the cat you are inspecting has daggerboards, checking the trunks where the boards go through the hulls is important. Look for cracks that might mean leakage. Ask the owner how much the boat leaks on a windy day. Most cats take on some water when they're pushed hard, so don't be put off by a little water in the hulls. The hulls are never air tight since they need to breathe to accommodate temperature variations. Any more than two cupfuls of water per day is reason to seriously inspect trunks and seams for leaks. Also check the seals on *through-hull fittings* such as hull pylons and gudgeons.

LEARNING THE BASICS

CHECKING FOR LEAKS

A vacuum cleaner and a bucket of soapy water are the items you need for leak testing. Hook up the vacuum hose to the exit of the vacuum so it will blow air. Then put the hose end near the drain plug opening on one of the hulls to pressurize the

NACRA 6.0	
LENGTH OVERALL	20'
BEAM	8'6"
WEIGHT	420 LBS.
MAST HEIGHT	31'7"
SAIL AREA	264 SQ. FT.

SHOPPING AROUND
FOR A CAT

hull. Use caution here since only 4 pounds per square inch can do serious damage. Hold the hose in place while wiping all the seams and fitting areas with the soapy water. If bubbles begin to appear, you've got leaks. Most leaks are easy to repair with a small amount of marine silicone sealant. Small cracks and gaps can be repaired with marine epoxy putty.

THE SPARS

The aluminum *spars* on cats may not look like much, but they're expensive, so make sure you sight along each spar and check for straightness. A bent spar should be replaced. Also, check the rigging—all the wires on the mast—and look for rust, fraying, and poor *swedging*. A bad swedge fitting (the metal rings that hold the shrouds at their ends) can lead to dismasting.

If the wires or swedges are suspect, don't worry about it. These items are not too expensive and should be replaced

INTER 18
LENGTH OVERALL 18'1"
BEAM 8'6"
WEIGHT 374 LBS.
MAST HEIGHT 29'6"
SAIL AREA 227.7 SQ. FT.

LEARNING THE BASICS

every few years anyway. Check the *chainplates* where the shrouds are held to the deck or hull. Are they loose or cracked? If so, this will involve fiberglass work for their replacement—and that runs into money.

INTER 20
LENGTH OVERALL   20'
BEAM   8'6"
WEIGHT   390 LBS.
MAST HEIGHT   32'
SAIL AREA   246 SQ. FT.

SAILS AND TRAMPOLINE

Sails should be rolled out on the floor and thoroughly inspected for wear. Check all the corners and batten pockets for tears. Minor rips are easily repaired, so what you want to know is if you'll have to soon replace the whole sail—again an expensive item.

The age of a sail can be estimated by its color and texture. A yellow or faded sail has been around for a few years at least. The thing you're really interested in is how much resin is left in the sail—this determines longevity. Check for resin left in the cloth by grabbing a bunch of the sail in your hands and squeezing it. A soft smooth sail is usually a well-used sail. If the material still has some crispness to it, it's probably good for a few more seasons at least. With Kevlar or Mylar sails look for cracks in the cloth; too many cracks means it's time for a new sail.

Like sails, trampolines are also expensive and need to be examined closely. Again, age is your main concern here. If many of the grommets are loose and ripping out, you can count on replacing the trampoline soon. Also, remember that a brittle, sun-baked trampoline will not withstand repair—so determine its condition. If the trampoline is supple and not too bleached out, small rips can be repaired. But a rip in a brittle trampoline usually leads to the purchase of a new one.

EXTRA GEAR

The purchase of a cat is seldom the end to dipping in to your wallet. There are always those small things that can make sailing a little more enjoyable. While this book is not intended to be a consumer guide on cat goodies, the items listed here are worthy of consideration.

DAYSAILING ESSENTIALS

1. Life jackets. Comfortable ones that will remain so after a few hours.
2. Sun protection. Sunglasses and a visor.
3. Lip protector. A commercial lip balm.
4. Wet suit or foul weather gear. If you plan to be sailing in cold weather, surfing wetsuits are excellent. Wear shorts over the bottom of your wetsuit to protect it from chafing. And make sure the wetsuit is light and supple, allowing for easy movement.
5. Righting line. (A rope used to help right the cat after a capsize.) This is a must and it should be thick enough so that it is easy to get a grip on.
6. A small ditty bag. One that contains tools, extra shackles, sponge, duct tape, (for quick repairs of the sail or hulls) pins and rings for the rigging.
7. Non-skid or carpet for the deck or sidebars.

DAYSAILING OPTIONS

1. Cooler for food and drinks.
2. Rigging knife.
3. Padded hiking straps or booties. Comfortable straps or rubberized booties can really save you a lot of pain on a windy day.
4. Padded trapeze harnesses.
5. Sailing gloves.

RACING ESSENTIALS

1. Good sail(s) (see chapter 10).
2. Fast-action trapeze unit(s) (see chapter 8).
3. Good blocks and cleats.
4. Sailing gloves.
5. Righting line.
6. Wetsuit or foul weather gear.
7. Quick batten tension adjusters (see chapter 6).
8. Non-skid for trapezing.
9. Booties or padded hiking straps.
10. Good rudders and boards.
11. Waterproof stopwatch.
12. Masthead or bridle fly (see chapter 4).
13. Small ditty bag for spare parts.
14. Padded trapeze harnesses (see chapter 8).

RACING OPTIONS

1. Boomvang (see chapter 9).
2. Pulley-type trapeze rig (see chapter 8).
3. Windows in sails for tell-tales (see chapter 9).
4. Adjustable tiller extension.
5. Rigging knife.
6. Compass.

SHOPPING AROUND
FOR A CAT

2\
ANATOMY
OF A
CATAMARAN

To thoroughly enjoy your cat and the sailing experience, you'll need to recognize by name and understand all the parts on your boat. Not knowing your cat's anatomy leads to frustration for you, your crew, and your dealer.

Imagine walking in to a catamaran shop and telling the dealer, "I want to fix the thingamajig that rolls, the thing that a

The Hobie Cat, complete with its creator, Hobie Alter at the helm.

Figure 1

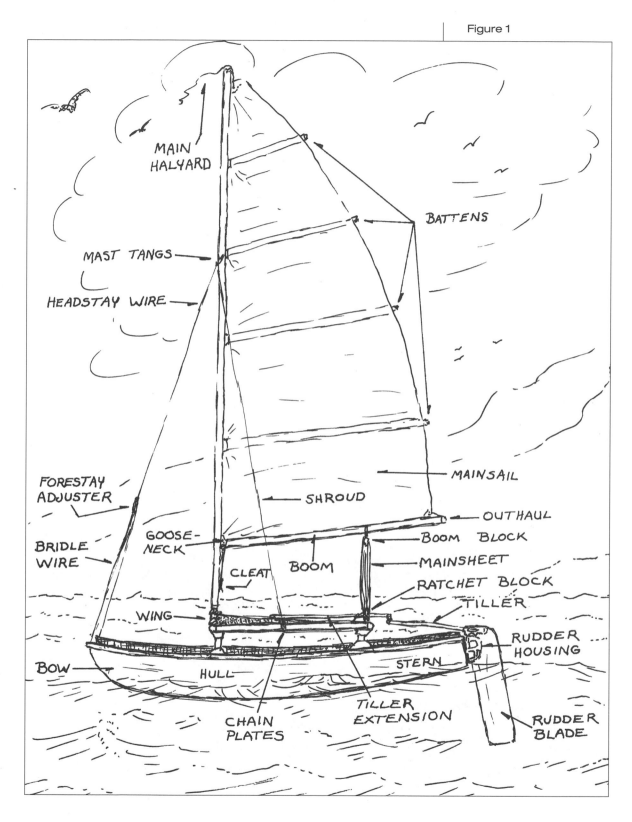

MAIN HALYARD

BATTENS

MAST TANGS

HEADSTAY WIRE

FORESTAY ADJUSTER

BRIDLE WIRE

GOOSE-NECK

CLEAT

WING

BOW

HULL

CHAIN PLATES

SHROUD

BOOM

TILLER EXTENSION

MAINSAIL

OUTHAUL

BOOM BLOCK

MAINSHEET

RATCHET BLOCK

TILLER

STERN

RUDDER HOUSING

RUDDER BLADE

ANATOMY OF A CATAMARAN

line runs through near the back of the boat—you know—that arched-shaped thing that runs along the. . .and ties to the. . .?" What a mess! Wouldn't it have been easier to have said: "Something is wrong with my traveler car—can you check it for me?" So, know thy cat!

THE BASIC CAT

The simplest cat is rigged with one mast and one sail, like a Hobie 14. This rig is known as a una rig or a cat rig (figure 1).

The term rig refers to the number of masts, booms, sails and supporting wires on the cat.

If a cat has a second smaller sail in front of the mainsail, then it's known as a sloop rigged cat (figure 2). If you're just getting into cat sailing, it may be a good idea to sail the sloop without the jib for awhile. But remember that in a crowded or narrow harbor, the jib on a sloop rigged cat really helps the boat tack—so having the jib up may be necessary.

PRINDLE 19
LENGTH OVERALL   19'2.5"
BEAM   8'6"
WEIGHT   385 LBS.
MAST HEIGHT   30'3"
SAIL AREA   247 SQ. FT.

Figure 2

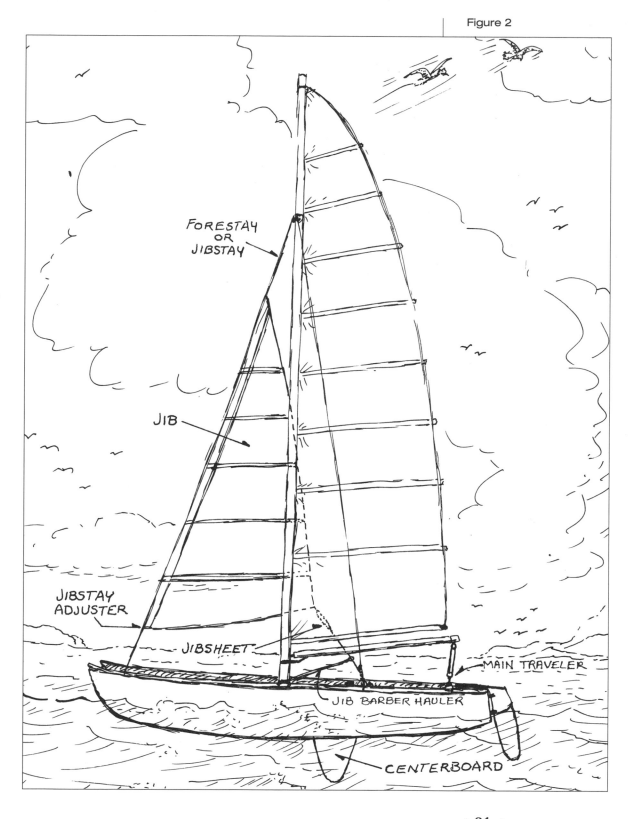

FORESTAY
OR
JIBSTAY

JIB

JIBSTAY
ADJUSTER

JIBSHEET

MAIN TRAVELER

JIB BARBER HAULER

CENTERBOARD

ANATOMY OF
A CATAMARAN

Figure 3

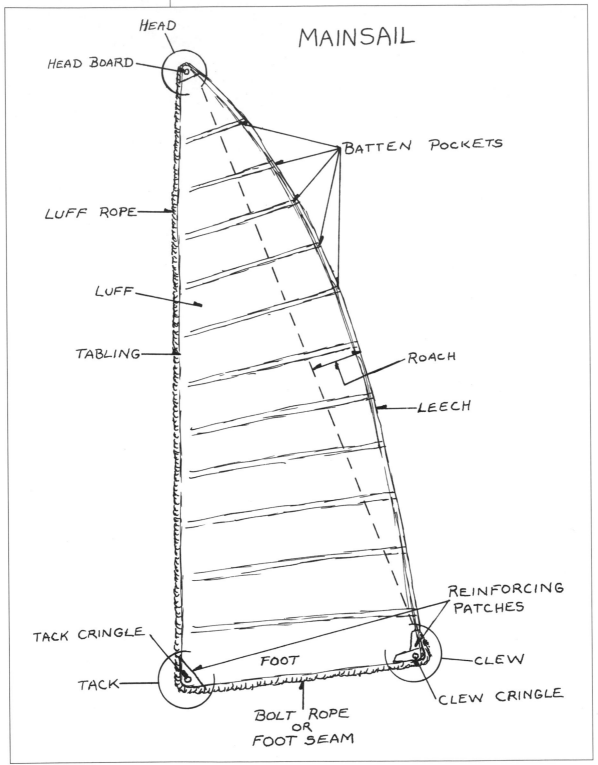

MAINSAIL

HEAD

HEAD BOARD

BATTEN POCKETS

LUFF ROPE

LUFF

TABLING

ROACH

LEECH

REINFORCING PATCHES

TACK CRINGLE

FOOT

CLEW

TACK

CLEW CRINGLE

BOLT ROPE
OR
FOOT SEAM

THE SAILS

Sails are your power source on a cat, so it's essential that you understand how they work. First, though, you've got to know terms connected with the sails (figure 3). Each corner and edge of a sail has a name. The forward or leading edge is called the *luff*. The bottom edge is called the *foot* and the outer edge is the *leech*. The top of the sail is called the *head*, and the plastic or metal plate that is attached to the head is called the *headboard*. The sail is pulled up the mast by the headboard—where the *halyard* attaches through a hole in it. The rear corner of the sail is the *clew*, and the bottom forward corner is the *tack*.

THE OUTHAUL AND DOWN HAUL

The *outhaul* is a line that pulls the bottom (foot) of the sail tight along the boom (figure 4). On *loose footed* rigs, (where the foot is not attached to the boom) the outhaul is very effective in adjusting foot tension for various wind strengths and points of sail.

On cats rigged with grooves or tracks on the boom to hold the sail along the foot, the outhaul is used to pull out wrinkles along the foot.

The *downhaul* is a line that pulls the boom down, which re-

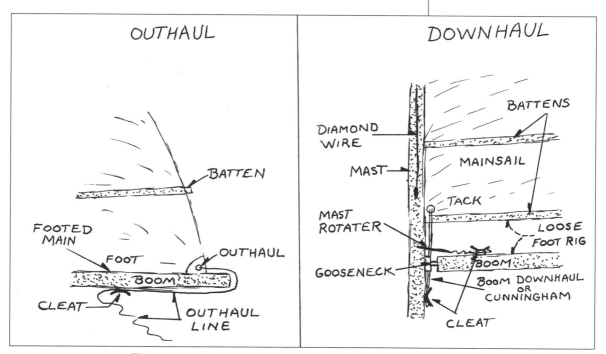

Figure 4

Figure 5

sults in tensioning the luff of the sail (figure 5). The downhaul is an important adjuster for sail shape (see chapter 11).

BATTENS

Battens are long strips of wood, fiberglass, or plastic. On cats, battens run "full length," from the leech to the luff of the mainsail and jib. Cats need a very uniform sail shape and battens create and hold this shape. Batten tension is the key to sail shape on a cat, with tighter batten tension creating a fuller sail. A full (deep pocket) sail increases the power of your rig, but makes sailing high into the wind difficult. Reduced batten tension has the opposite effect: not as much power, but a shape that will allow your cat to point into the wind higher (see chapter 11).

TRAVELERS AND BARBER-HAULERS

A traveler is a sail adjustment track that runs across the beam of a cat. It enables you to put a sail at a wider angle to the wind without having to release your sheet. Some cats have travelers for the main and the jib. Most have one just for the main, though. On cats without a jib traveler, another device that is often used is a barber-hauler. Basically, there is little difference in function between a jib traveler and barber-hauler.

A main traveler and mainsheet ratchet block.

SPARS AND RIGGING

The mast and boom are called *spars* and are usually joined together by a fitting called a *gooseneck*. The gooseneck slides into a groove in the mast.

There are two terms used in connection with rigging. *Standing rigging* refers to all the wires or shrouds used to support the mast. Most standing rigging on cats is made with strong 1x19 stainless wire. The wire is more than adequate to keep a mast up in almost all conditions, but the wire will break down if it is subjected to a lot of load-release action. This occurs if you leave a cat in the water with the mast up—each time a wake goes by, the mast jostles and the wire is jerked repeatedly. If you leave your cat in the water for a long time, either take the mast down or tension the shrouds with shock cord.

Running rigging is all the lines that are easily adjusted. *Halyards* and *sheets* are running rigging. Halyards are the lines that raise and lower sails. Sheets adjust sails out or in, laterally. The halyard that pulls up the mainsail is the *main halyard*, and the sheet that trims the mainsail is the *mainsheet*.

HELM

The helm is the mechanism that steers the boat. On a cat, you can steer from the *tiller crossbar* (the rod that connects the two rudders) or the *tiller extension* (the thin rod attached to the middle of the tiller crossbar). Most cat sailors prefer to steer

This helmsman is steering, sheeting, and sitting properly on his cat. The crew is preparing to get out on the trapeze.

Figure 6

with the tiller extension, but in heavy winds the crossbar makes for more secure steering.

CENTERBOARDS AND DAGGERBOARDS

The vast majority of cats sailing today have asymmetrical hulls, a hull form that keeps them from slipping sideways without the use of centerboards or daggerboards.

But many cats, including the flat-out racing cats, have symmetrical hulls that need boards to prevent sideslip (figure 6). A centerboard is either a wood, glass, or metal board that slides through a slot in the middle of a hull called a centerboard trunk. Centerboards pivot up and down in their trunks. Daggerboards, in contrast, go up and down in their trunks. Most racing cats have daggerboards since they don't require the trunk size that centerboards do, and this simplifies construction and reduces underwater disturbance. Either arrangement is satisfactory, however, and cats with boards are usually better upwind over their asymmetrical sisters.

3/
THE SAILING CIRCLE

Unlike a powerboat, a sailboat cannot always head directly to its destination. If the wind is blowing from the place you want to go, you have to have a good idea of how the wind affects you and your cat. Even when the wind is behind you, it's important to know the sailing circle to arrive at your destination safely (figure 1). A catamaran sailor must learn to recognize the wind direction at all times and how to set his sails in harmony with his steering to get to the places he wants to go.

There are five basic headings on the sailing circle. Whenever you go sailing, you can be sure you will have your cat on all of the headings at one time or another.

The five headings are: *close hauled* (or beating), *close reach, beam reach, broad reach* and *running*. If you are sailing on the left side of the circle, (where the wind crosses your cat's right or *starboard* side first) you are sailing on a starboard tack. And if you're sailing on the right side of the circle with the wind coming across your left or *port* side first, then you're on a port tack. So, there are ten general headings on the sailing circle; five on the starboard tack and five on the port tack.

Figure 1

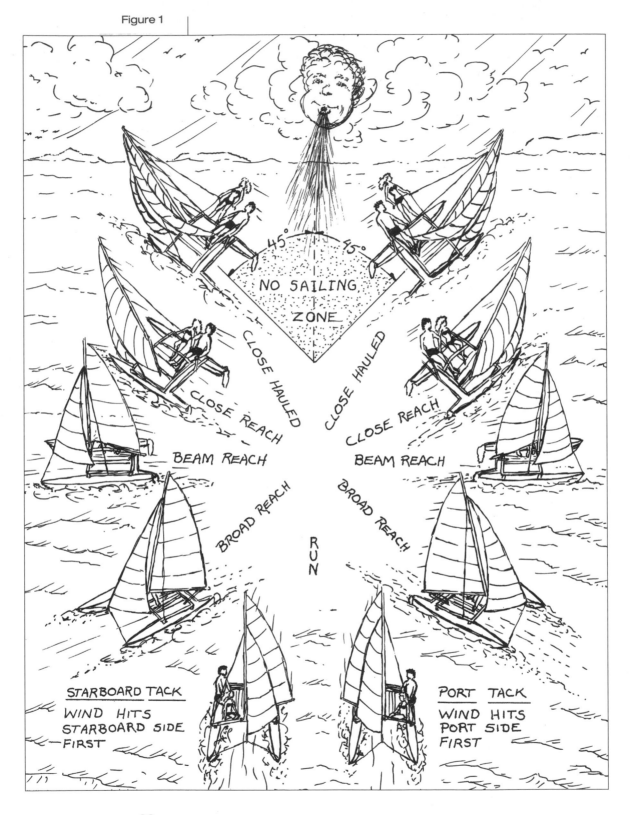

CLOSE HAULED

When a cat is being sailed as close to the wind as possible (around 45 degrees on port or starboard tack) it is sailing to *windward* or *close hauled*. When sailing to windward, the sails must be trimmed in tight, making for the term close hauled. This is often the most difficult point of sail for the beginner, since concentration and precise helming are needed to keep the cat moving forward and still pointing as close to the wind as possible.

If you are sailing back and forth (alternating from a close hauled starboard tack to a close hauled port tack) in an effort to arrive at a destination directly upwind, you are *beating to windward* (figure 2).

When you shift from a port tack to a starboard tack by turning the bows of your cat across the eye of the wind, you are *tacking*. When you are beating towards your destination, you may have to tack many times. Each time a tack is made, the boat must turn at least 90 degrees—from 45 degrees away from the wind on port tack to 45 degrees away from the wind on starboard tack, or vice versa. It takes practice and patience to tack a cat well—but once you have it down, it's easy. Tacking is covered in detail in chapter 5.

Figure 2

{REMEMBER: NEVER ABANDON SHIP EXCEPT IN EMERGENCIES!}

CAT BEATS TO WINDWARD IN A SERIES OF TACKS

REACHING

When a cat is being steered away from the wind (dropping down the sailing circle toward a run) from either a close hauled port tack or a close hauled starboard tack, it is beginning to reach. There are three basic reaches, *close reach*, *beam reach*, and *broad reach*.

The first reach as the boat heads away from the wind or *falls off,* is the close reach—about 50 to 85 degrees away from the eye of the wind. The close reach is an exciting point of sail, since most hull flying that cats do is done on this heading. When close reaching the sails are eased slightly from a close hauled setting because the more the boat falls off the wind, the more the back side of the sail is starved from wind flow if the sail is not let out. When the sail is let out to the right point on a reach, the wind will flow evenly on both sides of the sail— producing maximum power. Obviously then, the more you turn away from the wind towards a run, the more you must ease your sails to insure that you are getting proper wind flow across them.

This Prindle 16 is beam reaching at high speed. Note that the main traveler is out and the crew positioned aft.

LEARNING THE BASICS

When close reaching, either the traveler or the mainsheet or a combination of both are eased until proper trim is achieved. In sloop-rigged cats, the jib traveler or barber-hauler may need to be adjusted away from centerline as well (more on sail trim in chapters 4 and 9).

The second reach you come to as you fall off from a close reach is the *beam reach*. The beam reach (when the wind is approximately 90 degrees off the bows) is the fastest point of sail for a catamaran. The boat heels less and transforms energy wasted in hull-raising to forward thrust. When beam reaching, some cats, particularly Hobies, tend to stick their bows down into the water—which can lead to capsizing. This kind of "end-over-end" capsize is called *pitchpoling* and usually occurs in heavier winds. To avoid a pitch pole capsize, you must move your weight as far aft as possible and keep an eye on the leeward hull. When the hull begins to stick in or bury, you either have to *head up* towards the wind or ease sheets—quickly.

The wind blows directly across the cat's side when you are beam reaching, and the traveler should be eased out very far. If your cat has a traveler or barber-hauler for the jib, it should be trimmed way *outboard* as well. With the travelers in an outboard position the tension on the sheets can remain fairly tight. If you have a cat that doesn't have a traveler, then of course the sheets must be eased more than they would be normally.

The third reach on the sailing circle is the *broad reach*, about 100 to 160 degrees off the wind. The broad reach is a swift and stable point of sail. It is also the point of sail used by racers who choose to *tack downwind* instead of sail on a *dead run* (chapter 9). The tendency for a cat to pitch pole is usually reduced when you broad reach instead of beam reach. But, remember to keep an eye on that leeward bow in heavy air! The traveler remains in the full outboard position on the broad reach and the sheets are eased slightly from the beam reach setting.

RUNNING

As you continue to drop down the sailing circle and leave the broad reach, you end up on a *run*. The wind blows almost directly behind you on a run, and sheets are eased to let the boom out as far as it will go. A run is the slowest point of sail for a catamaran, and pitchpoling becomes less of a danger unless the wind is really howling. Another adjustment you can

This Hobie 18 is running. Note the slackened mainsheet and the crew positioned forward.

make on a run is to move your weight forward a little if it's not blowing too hard.

HELM AND HEADING

Style is important in sailing as it is in any other sport. When sailing your cat, always face the sail from the weather side of the boat. You want to be looking at the concave side of the sail at all times so that you can easily see when the sail needs trimming and then see the results of trimming. It's also important to steer with your backhand (closest to the stern) and trim the sheet with your forward hand (figure 3A). Unlike a car, a sailboat with a tiller heads the opposite way you steer it. Push left to go right (figure 3B), and push right to go left (figure 3C). The

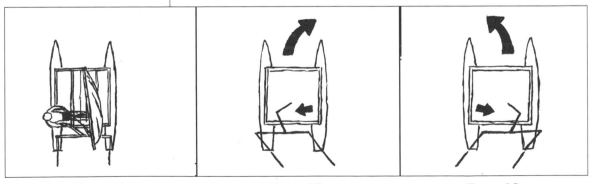

Figure 3A   Figure 3B   Figure 3C

LEARNING THE BASICS

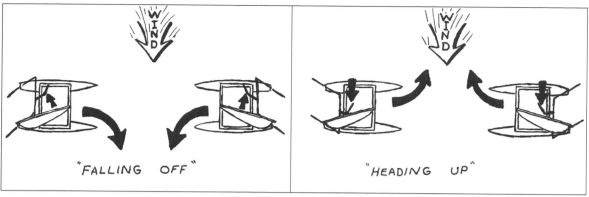

| Figure 4A | Figure 4B |

less wind you're sailing in, the slower the boat will react to steering. Helm sensitivity increases as speed picks up.

Whenever a sailboat changes direction, it is either *heading up* or *falling off*. The terms refer to the wind's angle to the boat. Heading up is when the boat turns closer to the eye of the wind and falling off is when the boat turns away from the wind.

If you are sitting on the windward side of your cat (facing the concave side of the sail) and you pull the tiller toward you, your boat will turn away from the wind—you are then falling off (figure 4A). Push the tiller away from you and your cat will turn towards the wind—you are heading up (figure 4B).

Generally, the closer you sail into the wind, (the more you head up) the closer your sails must be trimmed towards the centerline of your cat. And as you move away from the wind (fall off) the further the sails must be eased away from centerline. When sailing closehauled, your sails should be sheeted in tight. The secret to sailing closehauled then, is to know when to head up and fall off without adjusting your sails (chapter 4).

FINDING THE WIND

The most important thing to understand when you are sailing is where the wind is coming from at all times. After all, the wind dictates how you set your sails and often makes you sail in a direction other than a straight line towards your destination. Sailing is learning how to use the wind, and a good sailor never gets confused about wind direction.

But it is difficult for the beginner to determine the direction of the wind. The wind is an invisible force that most people normally pay little attention to. Illustrations present the wind

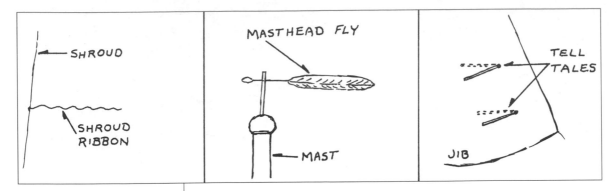

Figure 5

as an impersonal black arrow—we can see it, but it has no life. But when you're on the water in your cat, the wind has life—plenty of it—and if you can't read the wind, that life will make yours miserable!

Many sailors rely on senses other than their eyes to determine wind direction—mainly hearing and touch. They hear their sails luff and they feel the wind in their ears, on their cheeks and in their hair.

Instruments are also helpful and transmit the invisible power into something you can see. These include masthead flys (indicators on the tops of masts), yarn tied to the shrouds, tell-tales on the sails (ribbons attached to both sides of the sails) and bridle flys or vanes mounted on the forestay (figures 5 & 6).

Objects on shore such as flags, trees, and smoke are also helpful in determining wind direction. And on the water, other sailboats are your best indicators for wind shifts and fluctuations in velocity.

Good sailors use all of these indicators to help them sail their boats. Each time you go sailing it will become easier to read the wind—your mind will become a computer, taking in all the information from the various indicators and allowing you to get the most out of the wind and your boat. While good indicators on shore and on the water are not always available, you can have good indicators on your boat—it should be equipped with shroud yarns, a masthead, or bridle fly and tell-tales.

Figure 6

LEARNING THE BASICS

4/
GAINING
PROPER TRIM

To be a fast and safe cat sailor you have to work constantly toward the harmonization of three important variables: sail trim, steering, and body position. If this harmonization is not done—if the sails, for instance, are not set sympathetically in respect to body position, steering and the wind—all is lost.

Because this is true and since there is no such thing as a perfectly steady wind, course or heeling angle, the good catamaran sailor is always paying attention to these three variables.

CLEATS AND SHEETS

Before we dive into the essence of trim, steering, and body position, we should go over sheet handling. You can 't begin to trim a cat unless you're completely familiar with its sheeting system(s).

In a two-person cat, the helmsman handles the mainsheet while the crew is responsible for the jibsheets. It is crucial that the helmsman have his hand on the mainsheet at all times. The mainsail is much larger than the jib and its quick release in a sudden gust will often prevent a capsize. The mainsheet should be carried in your forward hand. If you need to drop the sheet for a moment, put it in your lap—where it can be found quickly. For the crew on the jibsheet, things aren't so crucial. In light air the crew may cleat the jib and drop the sheet until sail trim is needed.

In handling the jibsheet the crew should remember that there are two jibsheets (port and starboard) and only one sheet is used at one time—meaning that the other sheet should have plenty of slack so that it is not disturbing the trim of the jib.

CLEATING

Most cats have an "up to cleat, down to uncleat" sheeting system for the main and jib (figure 1). For making an adjustment to sail trim, the sheet is pulled taut, lifted up, then whipped quickly down with a flick of the wrist. The sheet is then free of the cleat and can be let out. For bringing the sail in, the sheet is simply pulled—without leaving the jaws of the cleat. While it's a little difficult to explain, the mechanics of sheet adjustment are simple to learn. The important thing is knowing how to work the sheeting system(s) on your cat before you go sailing. Ask your dealer or another sailor if you're unsure about

Figure 1

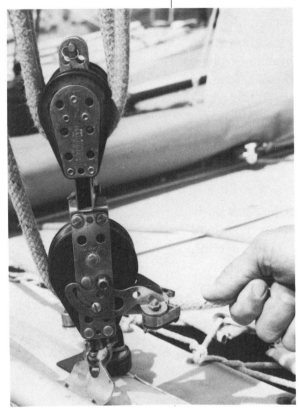

"Up to cleat"

"Down to uncleat"

LEARNING THE BASICS

the technique—then practice it. And remember the cardinal rule of cat sailing: "When in doubt, sheet out."

BALANCING

An important part of sailing your cat right is balancing. A well-balanced cat is fast because its hulls are at the right angle to go through the water with a minimum of drag, and the sails on a well-balanced cat are at the right angle to the wind—giving the most power. A cat with dragging sterns (from too much weight aft) or a cat that is heeled too far to leeward (from not moving your weight further outboard) is losing a lot of speed.

In balancing a cat there are two things to be concerned with: the degree of heel and the fore and aft balance. Heeling in a cat either to windward or to leeward is crucial to performance. For optimum sailing, a cat should have a slight heel to leeward (figure 2).

Remember that a cat should never have a great heel to leeward or any heel to windward. Both conditions make for slow sailing. As a rule, a cat should always be heeled slightly to leeward, except when running downwind. In light winds it is sometimes necessary to move your weight amidships to gain a

Hiking out on straps.

Figure 2

HEELING TO LEEWARD

WIND

HEELING TO WINDWARD

WIND

SAILING RIGHT

WIND

Hiking out on a trapeze.

slight leeward heel. If you're sailing on a two-man cat, the crew may have to sit well down to leeward to create heel—possibly on the leeward hull itself. The important thing to remember is that you don't want your cat heeling to windward. As the wind increases, crew weight should be gradually moved to windward to counteract the heeling force generated by the stronger wind. In heavy air, the crew on a cat must *hike out*. Hiking out is done from a pair of straps that run lengthwise across the trampoline. By putting your feet under the straps and hanging your butt(s) over the side, you provide good leverage for keeping that windward rail down.

On larger cats and on some one-man cats, a technique called trapezing is used to keep a cat on its feet. Trapezing is done from a wire that hangs from the mast which the crew

GAINING PROPER TRIM

hooks into while wearing a special harness. Standing on the windward rail with your body fully extended and hanging from a wire is one of the big thrills of cat sailing—and the most effective way to fight excessive leeward heel.

While hiking and trapezing go a long way in keeping your cat on her feet, there comes a point when a cat's crew can no longer keep the boat down. This is the time when you need to be very alert with the sheets ready to release them in a sudden gust. You can afford to relax in light or moderate winds, but when it begins blowing hard your alertness and ability to let the sails out quickly are the answers to staying dry and keeping your cat in an upright position! For details on trapezing and heavy air sailing, see chapter 8.

FORE AND AFT TRIM

A well-balanced cat usually has its sterns just off or level with the water; its bows, from deck level should be at least six inches off the water (figure 3). Unlike heel, there are no exact rules to follow—each cat requires its own fore and aft trim and it takes on-the-water experience to feel just what is needed.

Since most cats tend to lift their sterns and bury their bows on heavy air reaches, you must use crew weight to maintain correct balance. Whenever the bows begin to dig, weight must be moved aft. The more wind there is, the further aft your weight is needed. When sailing upwind the reverse is true, cats usually tend to lift their bows—requiring more weight forward as the sterns begin to depress.

Wind velocity also plays an important role in how you balance your cat. If it's really blowing, you may find that you must keep your weight well aft regardless of the point of sail you're

Figure 3

STERN HEAVY   CORRECT TRIM   BOW HEAVY

LEARNING THE BASICS

on. The opposite is usually true in light air, but the secret to good trim remains the same—you must always strive to keep your cat sailing level.

The surface of the water affects fore and aft trim too. In smooth water, it's easy to keep a cat level (unless it's really blowing). But in rough water, regardless of the wind, keeping proper fore and aft trim takes effort. If, for instance, you are sailing close hauled in light wind and rough water, you may have to sit well aft to keep the bows from plowing into the backs of waves. When surfing, shifting your weight at regular intervals forward and aft helps in catching waves—and also aids in avoiding a *"pearl"* into the back of other waves (for details on surfing, see chapter 14).

SAIL TRIM

The sails, which the sheets control, are your main source of power in a sailboat. Unless they are set at precisely the right angle to the wind at all times, they will not allow you to get the most out of your cat. It is not enough to simply judge wind direction and then adjust the sheets until things feel "right." More reliable methods are available for sail trimming and learning to use them is essential.

Good sail trim takes an eye for "reading the luff" of the sail(s) and the understanding that sail sheeting and helmsmanship are a dynamic relationship. Proper sail trim can be achieved two ways—either by altering your course to keep the sails at the right angle to the wind or by staying on the same course and altering your sail trim, by altering sheet tension.

SAILING BY THE LUFF

Since a perfectly steady course and wind do not exist, when sailors refer to steady sailing they mean "steady as she goes." This term applies to you, your helmsmanship, and to mother nature. Because of this, and the fact that the sails don't work well unless they are set at the right angles to the wind, windshifts and course changes demand sail trimming. But how can you tell how to adjust the sail(s) when a course change or a windshift occurs? The most common way is to watch the forward portion of the sail(s), the luff.

Whenever a sail is not pulled in tight enough and whenever you are sailing too close to the wind, the sail will *luff*. When you are sailing your boat right there is no luffing—the forward part of your sail is undisturbed, it is "full" of wind. But if the luff area is billowing out and appears convex instead of having its normal concave shape, you are luffing and something must be done.

There are two ways to stop the luffing: either change your course and *fall off* (away from) the wind, or trim your sails by bringing in the sheets or adjusting the traveler. A good way to picture the luffing situation is to think of the sail as a flag. If you pull the tail of the flag into or towards the wind, it fills with air and stops waving. Pulling the flag around towards the wind and holding it to stop its waving is like trimming in sails. And as you gradually ease the flag, it begins to wave again as it lines up with the wind. If you gradually ease your sail, it will begin luffing as it lines up with the wind.

SAILING ON A STEADY COURSE

Watching the luff is the key to trimming sails on a steady-as-she-goes course. If you are unsure about how your sail is trimmed, ease it out until it begins to luff then bring it back in

Figure 4

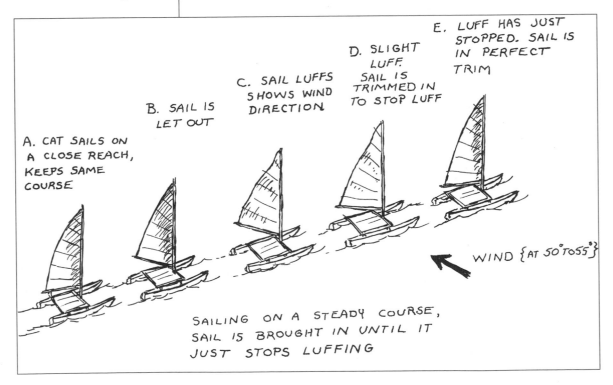

A. CAT SAILS ON A CLOSE REACH, KEEPS SAME COURSE

B. SAIL IS LET OUT

C. SAIL LUFFS SHOWS WIND DIRECTION

D. SLIGHT LUFF. SAIL IS TRIMMED IN TO STOP LUFF

E. LUFF HAS JUST STOPPED. SAIL IS IN PERFECT TRIM

WIND {AT 50° TO 55°}

SAILING ON A STEADY COURSE, SAIL IS BROUGHT IN UNTIL IT JUST STOPS LUFFING

LEARNING THE BASICS

just to the point where the luffing stops (figure 4). If the wind begins to shift more in front of you, the sheet(s) must be brought in until the sail stops luffing. If the wind shifts more behind you, the sail(s) will not luff but they will be in too tight. Tell-tales on the sail(s) help in determining if you're over-sheeted (chapter 9). Remember, if you think you're oversheeted and your sail is in too tight, ease the sheet out until the sail begins to luff—then bring it back in until the luffing stops.

SAILING ON AN UNSTEADY COURSE

If holding a steady course is not important and you're feeling lazy, you can keep your sails trimmed properly by altering your course instead of adjusting the sheets. You can also deal with windshifts this way. If the wind shifts behind you, you can head up (towards the wind) instead of letting your sheets out (figure 5). If the wind isn't shifting and you change course, then you'll have to adjust your sails (figure 6).

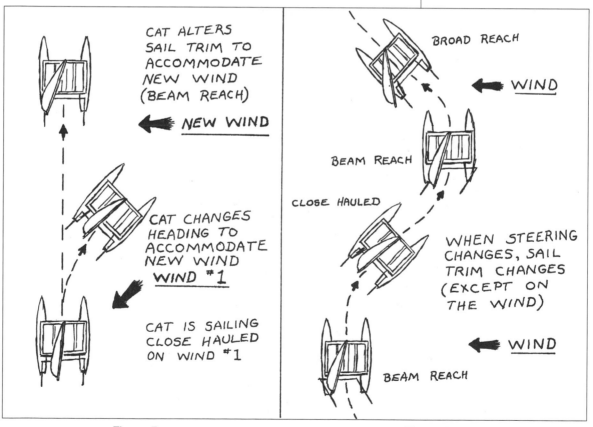

Figure 5   Figure 6

SAILING CLOSEHAULED

While the emphasis is on trimming sails when you are on a steady-as-she-goes course "off the wind," you must sail differ-

Figure 7

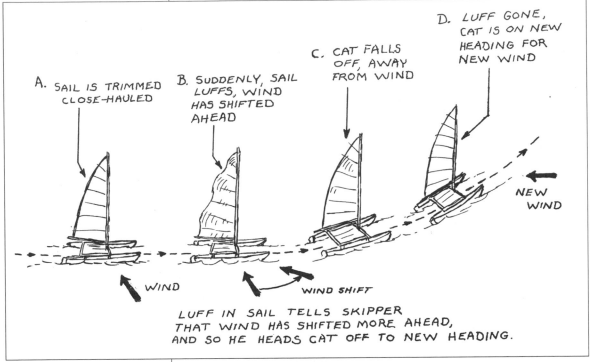

A. SAIL IS TRIMMED CLOSE-HAULED

B. SUDDENLY, SAIL LUFFS, WIND HAS SHIFTED AHEAD

C. CAT FALLS OFF, AWAY FROM WIND

D. LUFF GONE, CAT IS ON NEW HEADING FOR NEW WIND

NEW WIND

WIND

WIND SHIFT

LUFF IN SAIL TELLS SKIPPER THAT WIND HAS SHIFTED MORE AHEAD, AND SO HE HEADS CAT OFF TO NEW HEADING.

These G-cats are sailing upwind—note the tightly trimmed-in sails.

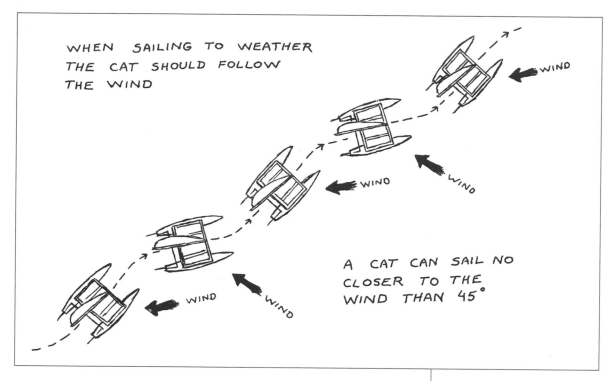

WHEN SAILING TO WEATHER THE CAT SHOULD FOLLOW THE WIND

WIND

WIND

WIND

WIND

WIND

A CAT CAN SAIL NO CLOSER TO THE WIND THAN 45°

Figure 8

ently when you're sailing "on the wind" or closehauled. Since the sails are sheeted in tight on a closehauled course, they can no longer be trimmed in when they begin to luff. Thus, the job of keeping the *sails full* falls to good helmsmanship. When the jib begins to luff the skipper can no longer yell to his crew, "sheet in the jib!"—because it's sheeted in as far as it will go. If the sail is luffing, the skipper must fall off by steering the boat away from the wind (figure 7). Sometimes a skipper falls away from the wind too far when correcting for luffing and this results in a badly trimmed boat because the sheets are in too tight. To avoid this, the skipper must head towards the wind again, just to the point of luffing. And so it goes—sailing to windward takes constant testing—heading up to see how far you can go before the sail luffs, then falling off again to fill the sail completely. A catamaran must be worked to weather in a series of *scallops*—heading up and then falling off—to keep the boat sailing fast and as close to the eye of the wind as possible (figure 8).

FOOTING AND PINCHING

As your helmsmanship skills increase, you will realize that there are two ways to sail closehauled. You can constantly push

Figure 9

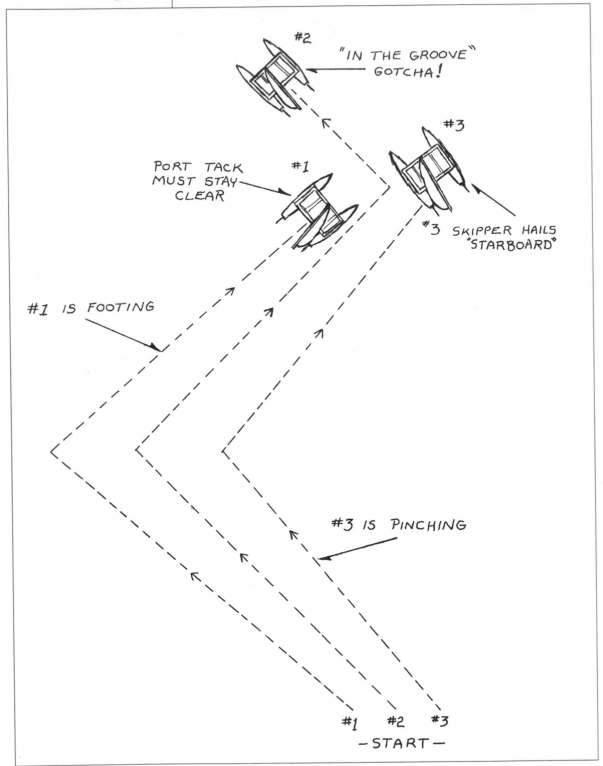

#2 "IN THE GROOVE" GOTCHA!

#3

PORT TACK MUST STAY CLEAR   #1

#3 SKIPPER HAILS "STARBOARD"

#1 IS FOOTING

#3 IS PINCHING

#1   #2   #3

—START—

your cat to sail as close to the wind as possible (always on the verge of luffing) or, you can sail further off the wind (still sailing closehauled, but never close to luffing). If you sail your cat as close to the wind as possible, sacrificing speed to do so, you are *pinching*. If it's speed you're after and you're willing to sacrifice sailing close to the wind in order to go faster, then you're *footing*. Both footing and pinching are techniques that racing sailors use, depending on what they need to get out of their cat at a given time. Beginners tend to pinch too much when they are sailing closehauled—which results in slow sailing. The best way to sail to weather is to find a happy medium between footing and pinching. When you find this medium, you are "sailing in the groove"—just right (figure 9).

Note: As you begin, sail your cat with its main traveler near center and its jib traveler or barber hauler inboard. This lets you concentrate on the basics and makes reading the luff(s) easier. (See chapter 9 for more on travelers.)

5/
CHANGING TACKS

The sailing circle shows that whenever a boat is sailing, it is either on a port or starboard tack. Sooner or later, a boat has to change from one tack to another, and there are two ways to do it: tacking or jibing.

| Figure 1 | Figure 2 |

Tacking is when the bows of your cat turn up through the eye of the wind; you are turning towards the wind. Jibing is the opposite; your cat is turning away from the wind—instead of the bows crossing the eye of the wind, your sterns are crossing. Both maneuvers require practice and concentration at first, then they become easier and easier to do. Good cat sailors don't even think about tacking or jibing—the maneuvers are done automatically. But the beginner must practice before tacking and jibing become natural. And before practicing, one must know the fundamentals.

If you pull the tiller toward your body (fall off) for an extended period of time, you will eventually jibe. The wind is behind you during a jibe, which means that the sterns of your cat and the leech of your mainsail are passing through the eye of the wind during the maneuver (figure 1).

When you push the tiller away from you (head up) for an extended period of time, you will eventually tack (if you keep proper sheet trim and rudder angle). As you tack you are turning into the wind; your bows and the luff of your mainsail are passing through the eye of the wind as you change tacks (figure 2).

Note the boomless mainsails, which are growing more popular due to their simplicity and weight savings.

JIBING

More sailors get into trouble when trying to jibe than at any other time. Really though, jibing is easy if you remember certain steps and practice them. You can't just fall off the wind and duck your head as the boom comes flying across. Neither can you simply grab the boom and pull it across your boat to the other side.

Jibing correctly will save you from an unexpected swim or a bash in the head by the boom. Doing it right is knowing when to do what.

First, you have to be sure that the wind is blowing almost dead astern. To check the wind take a look at your shroud yarns, bridle vane, or masthead fly. When you're first learning to jibe you have to be sailing almost dead downwind—otherwise you'll be learning how to right your boat too!

If you have a crew, make sure you tell them in advance of your plans to jibe. This lets your crew get prepared—remember, your crew can't read your mind. The simple hail of "prepare to jibe" should tell your crew all he/she needs to know.

Just before jibing, you should face aft and place one hand

Figure 3

Figure 4

Figure 5

Figure 6

LEARNING THE BASICS

on the tiller (figure 3). If your cat has a single tiller extension, you may want to swing it across to the other side prior to the jibe. By swinging the tiller extension around in advance you'll have instant control of your cat right after jibing. Just after swinging the tiller extension around, grab each of the lines that make up the mainsheet system about a foot down from the boom—now you're ready for the jibe (figure 4). Turn sharply towards your new tack and pull the boom across with the mainsheet system. By pulling the mainsheet across all at once, you control the boom swing and keep the sheet from getting tangled. Remember to duck your head during all of this to avoid the boom, which might come swinging across the cat very fast (figure 5).

Once the mainsail is across, your crew can uncleat the jib and trim it to match the trim of the main on your new tack. Then it's time to move your weight across to the other side of the trampoline and resume sitting in the correct sailing position (figure 6).

SAILING BY THE LEE

When you are sailing downwind and the wind begins to blow over the same side of the cat that the sails are on, you are "sailing by the lee." Sailing by the lee is a risky point of sail for all

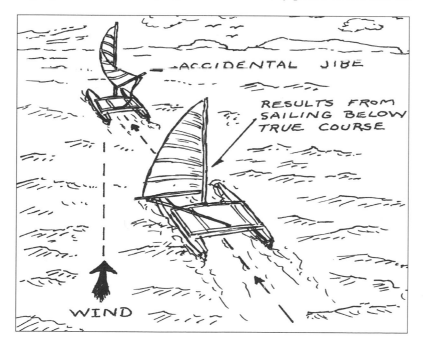

Figure 7

but the very experienced because the chances of an accidental jibe are high (figure 7). One sign of an approaching jibe is the boom rising and the upper part of the mainsail leech collapsing or fluttering. If you suddenly feel a jibe coming on, the only thing you can do is head up quickly towards the wind. If it looks like you're going to jibe anyway, be sure to duck your head!

Some skippers like to sail by the lee with the mainsail and jib on opposite sides. This is known as sailing "wing and wing" because the boat seems to have wings with its sails reaching out to port and starboard. While wing and wing sailing might look nice, most experienced cat sailors seldom sail this way (chapter 9).

TACKING

While most catamarans are faster than monohulls, they are not as maneuverable. One maneuver that cats are famous for doing slowly is tacking.

Cats tack slower than monohulls for good reason—their long fine hulls, that are spread far apart, resist short radius turning. Cats are also very light and therefore slow down quickly when being turned into the wind. But, cats do tack, and they are easy to tack—once you get the hang of it. Tacking a cat requires a subtle approach to helmsmanship and body movement.

TACKING THE SLOOP-RIGGED CAT

1. Hail to the crew, "prepare to tack."
2. Instruct your crew to leave the jib cleated until you ask for it to be released.
3. Do not begin a tack from a reach. Always make sure you are sailing closehauled before tacking.
4. Make sure you have plenty of speed—the most you can generate for the wind and sea conditions.
5. Make sure your crew is in all the way from the trapeze—only experts will try tacking while the crew is still out on the wire.
6. To begin your tack, push the tiller firmly so that your cat makes a *gradual* turn. Never push the tiller quickly or all the way over. Such rudder movements kill speed—and your tack. Most of the time you need only half the rudder throw that is available (figure 8).

7. As the bows of your cat turn into the eye of the wind, you and your crew must move across the boat (figure 9). The best way to move across the trampoline is to stay on your feet or knees—don't drag yourself or slide across. And while you are moving, you should also be swinging the tiller around the back of the boat so it is ready to use on the new tack.

8. After moving to the other side of the cat, you should have switched hands on the mainsheet and tiller—and should be starting to straighten the boat out on course (figure 10).

9. As soon as the mainsail fills on the new tack and the mast has rotated, you should tell your crew to "cut the jib" and he/she can then trim it to the other side (figure 11). It is important to hold onto the jib through

Figure 8

Figure 9

Figure 10

Figure 11

the tack and let it *backwind*. By letting the jib catch the wind on its "back side" you are insuring that your bows will swing through the wind.

Note: To aid mast rotation it's sometimes necessary to ease the mainsail about a foot when crossing the eye of the wind. If this doesn't work, the crew can either push or kick the aft edge of the mast until it rotates. Remember, a counter rotated mast makes for slow sailing.

TACKING THE UNA RIG

Learning to tack the una-rigged cat is difficult even for advanced sailors (this is especially true for Hobie 14 sailors). The una rig does not have a jib to back wind, so it must rely entirely on its own momentum to carry it up through the eye of the wind. Only practice will lead to fast taking this rig, and here are the steps to follow:

1. Before tacking, you must be moving at full speed on a close-hauled tack. Never tack from a reach—even a close reach (figure 12).
2. Like the sloop tack, push the tiller firmly but gradually so the cat makes a moderate turn. Don't shove the tiller fast or hard over—use about half of the rudder throw that is available.
3. Once into the turn, move smoothly aft—but without disturbing your hull trim. And as you move aft, make sure you are keeping the rudders turned the right amount (figure 13).
4. As your cat moves into the wind, let out 8 to 12 inches of your mainsheet. Then, in almost the same movement, pass the tiller 180 degrees around and knee walk across the trampoline (figure 14).
5. When the mast begins to tilt over to the opposite position on the new tack, and the bows have swung through the eye of the wind, straighten out the rudders and sheet the mainsail back in (figure 15).
6. Trim the hulls (figure 16).

Note: One thing to keep in mind is that if you don't cross the boat quickly enough, it may surprise you and start flying a hull. If you find this happening, let the sheet out and get to the windward side fast!

Figure 12

Figure 13

Figure 14

Figure 15

Figure 16

CHANGING TACKS

THE DON'TS OF CATAMARAN TACKING

1. Don't tack from a reach.
2. Don't tack until you are moving as fast as you can in the existing conditions.
3. Don't tack while the crew is out on the trapeze—unless you've really got it down.
4. Don't push the tiller hard over.
5. Don't jump around when crossing to the other side of the trampoline—keep your movements fluid.
6. Don't leave the mainsheet in tight unless the mast can rotate easily.
7. Don't scull (pump the rudders back and forth). If you're sculling during your tacks, you're doing something wrong.
8. Don't sheet the sails in hard and quick after a tack. If your cat is not quite all the way around, sheeting in too soon will put you in irons.
9. Don't sail with a counter rotated mast.
10. Don't try to tack when you are "flying a hull."

POPPING THE BATTENS

In very light winds the battens in the sail(s) may not "pop over" to the correct curve after a tack. If they remain bowed to windward, they will either kill your speed or keep you from completing your tack. To get the mainsail battens on the right side, just push the boom away from your body and then rapidly pull it back towards you. A quick push pull should do the trick. To pop a jib, the clew should be pushed and pulled until the battens pop to the right side.

GETTING THE SLOOP RIG OUT OF IRONS

When, for one reason or another, you blow a tack and end up with your cat dead into the wind with no speed, you are in *irons*. Being in irons is really not as criminal as it sounds—and unlike the prison variety, sailing irons are easy to get out of:

1. The crew should haul the jib to the opposite side you want to turn towards (figure 17).
2. The tiller must be pushed hard over so that it is pointing in the direction you want to go.

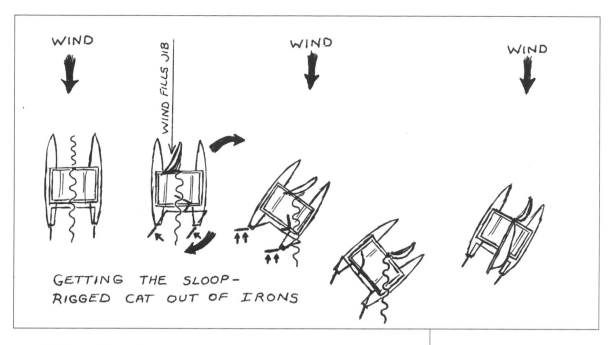

WIND

WIND FILLS JIB

WIND

WIND

GETTING THE SLOOP-
RIGGED CAT OUT OF IRONS

Figure 17

3. Keep the weight balanced and amidships.
4. Keep the mainsheet loose.

After doing these things, the wind will hit the jib and create both a turning and pushing action. The rudders will act as a brake which assists the bows in swinging towards the new tack.

5. Once the bows have swung away from the wind enough, the backwinded jib can be let loose, the rudders slowly straightened, and the sails gradually trimmed in.

These steps will get you out of irons provided you do each one properly. If you forget a step or don't do one right, you'll remain in irons until you figure out what you're doing wrong. Here are a few things most beginning cat sailors are guilty of when trying to get out of irons:

1. Not allowing the bows to swing off the wind enough before trying to sail. Remember, closehauled is 45 degrees away from the eye of the wind.
2. Sheeting in the main too quickly. Remember, your cat has to be completely on the other tack at least 45 degrees away from the wind before you can sheet in the mainsail.
3. Straightening out the tiller and stalling the cat before it has a chance to get going again.

GETTING THE UNA CAT OUT OF IRONS

When you find yourself in irons on an una—rigged cat, either stand or sit up high on your knees near the stern and push the boom and the tiller in the direction you want to go (figure 18). You only need to push the boom to the point where the after edge of the sail catches some wind. Remember to have the tiller pushed hard over during this maneuver—you will be going slowly backwards and turning at the same time.

As you go backwards the bows will be swinging away from the wind. When the bows have swung at least 45 degrees from the eye of the wind you can move forward, straighten out the rudders, and sheet in the sail. The important thing to grasp here is that the bows must swing at least 45 degrees off the wind—otherwise, you'll be back in irons.

Figure 18

GETTING THE UNA RIG
OUT OF IRONS

6/
RIGGING
FOR A SAIL

When you first go through the ritual of rigging your cat for sailing it seems like a complicated task that robs you of time on the water. Soon though, you'll develop your own ways of stepping the mast, rigging up, and hoisting sail. Before long, rigging

for sail will happen almost automatically, taking little time. But to get to this point you have to know the basic steps for rigging outlined in this chapter—beginning with stepping the mast.

STEPPING THE MAST

If your cat has a light or short mast, then stepping it is fairly simple by using the "straight lift" method of stepping. A long or heavy mast requires a hinge at its base and usually takes two people for stepping.

Before you begin, however, there are a couple of things to consider. First, take a look above you. Several sailors have been killed in recent years when their masts hit overhead wires while they were holding onto their boats. If there are any wires around the area, don't take a chance—step your mast after you get your cat near the water. Also, make sure there is plenty of room for stepping. You need at least 20 feet behind your cat, or whatever distance your mast covers when it's resting on the trampoline ready to be raised.

STEPPING A HINGED MAST

1. Untie the mast, shrouds and stays from your cat and trailer. The masthead should be facing aft.
2. Make sure the shrouds, trapeze wires and forestay wires are securely attached to the mast. They should be attached in the following order: (figure 1).
   a. left trapeze wire(s)
   b. left shroud
   c. forestay
   d. right shroud
   e. right trapeze wire(s)
3. Be sure to tighten up all your tang shackles with a shackle tool or a pair of pliers. Then secure the safety wire that keeps the shackle pin from working loose.
4. Attach the right and left shrouds (if not already attached) to their respective chainplates (figure 2).
5. Place the mast pivot bearing or teflon chip into the mastbase cup (figure 3).
6. Shift the mastbase aft until it's resting near the mast-step (figure 4). Then fasten the mastbase to the mast-step by attaching the hinge components (figure 5).

LEARNING THE BASICS

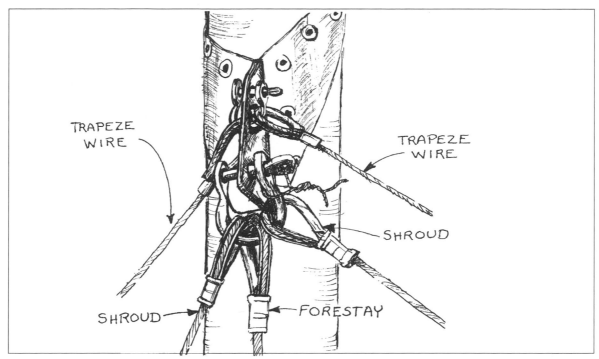

Figure 1

Figure 2

Figure 3

Figure 4

7. Now, the strongest person around should hop on the deck or trampoline and get ready to lift the mast.
8. Things can be made easier if someone at the masthead lifts the mast and gradually walks forward holding it as high as he can. While he's walking forward the person on deck is also raising the mast (figure 6). And, if there is someone else around, he/she can be on the alert for any rigging that might catch under the cat as the mast goes up (figure 7).

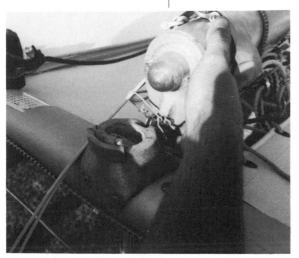

Figure 5

Figure 6

Figure 7

Figure 8

LEARNING THE BASICS

9. After the mast is up, hold it in place by putting forward pressure on it. Then the forestay can be attached by the person on the ground (figure 8).

10. After the forestay is attached, the hinge gear can be removed.

11. Attach all trapeze shock cords and tighten any shackles on the trapeze rig.

For downrigging, simply reverse these steps. If you store your cat on its trailer without removing its mast, you can avoid steps 2 and 4 since the shrouds, stays, and trapeze wires can be neatly coiled and stored on top of your cat when the mast is left lying on deck.

STRAIGHT LIFT STEPPING

After following steps 1 through 5 for stepping a hinged mast, follow these steps:

1. Check for tangled wires. Then stand on the trampoline or deck and grasp the mast near its center (figure 9).

2. Raise the mast until it is upright with its base resting on the ground in between the hulls and in front of the forward crossbar (figure 10).

Figure 9

Figure 10

Figure 11

Figure 12

3. Lift the mast straight up and try to keep it from angling away from you as you raise it. Once it's up plant the mastbase into the mastcup on the crossbar (figure 11).

4. After the mast is up and secure in the mastbase the forestay can be attached to the bridle chainplate by a friend (figure 12). If you're alone, you have to do some fancy footwork. Some solo sailors use an extended main halyard which they run through the bridle and back to the mast cleat. This system prevents the mast from falling back while you're trying to attach the forestay. Just after the mast is raised the line is tightened and cleated off, making for easy forestay attachment.

HOISTING SAILS

One of sailing's cardinal rules is never hoist a sail unless the bow of the boat is pointed directly into the wind. Ocean racing sailors don't follow this rule since they are often underway when they must make a sail change. But most catamaran sailors don't have to worry about changing sails while sailing. So remember, things will go a lot easier if your cat's bows are headed into the wind when raising sail. By being into the wind you also reduce the risk of a shoreside capsize.

Although cat rigging varies from class to class, the following steps for raising the mainsail and jib are applicable to most cats. For more detailed rigging instruction, see chapter 11.

HOISTING THE MAIN

1. Thread the foot of the mainsail through the boom by inserting the clew corner first and pulling the sail to the end of the boom (figure 13). On loose footed rigs you don't thread the sail through the boom—you just attach the clew to the end of the boom. Since cat mainsails are rolled and stored on booms, this step does not have to be repeated unless you take the sail off for repair.

2. Attach the tack to the gooseneck shackle at the front of the boom (figure 14).

3. Thread the outhaul line. The line is attached to the clew and should be run around the groove on the end of the boom (or through the pulley). Then pass the line under the mainsheet block hangers and cleat if off on the jam cleat that is on the boom (figure 15). Pull the outhaul just enough so the wrinkles along the bottom of the sail disappear. On loose-footed mains set the outhaul so that the curve at the bottom panel of the sail resembles the curve of the rest of the sail (see chapter 11 for detail).

Figure 13   Figure 14   Figure 15

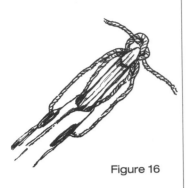

Figure 16

4. Before raising the mainsail make sure all of the battens are tied in their pockets securely. Use a square knot for this job (see figure 16 or Knots). If you have a set of batten tension adjusters, set them securely at the tension you wish by jamming the ties into the cleats (figures 17 A & B).

5. Attach the head of the sail to the main halyard with a shackle (figure 18). Be sure the halyard is not caught or twisted aloft. If there is a problem, flipping the cat on her side is often the easiest way to get at the problem (figure 19).

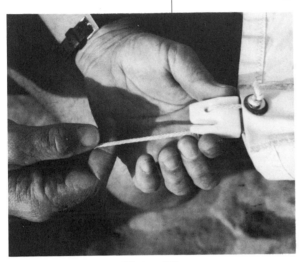

Figure 17A

Figure 17B

Figure 18

Figure 20

LEARNING THE BASICS

RETRIEVING A RUNAWAY HALYARD

Figure 19

6. Insert the top of the luff rope into the bottom of the luff groove on the mast. Then, as you feed the luff rope into the groove, raise the halyard (figure 20).

To make hoisting easier, rub the luffrope with paraffin wax or spray it on with a greaseless silicone lubricant.

As you hoist the sail, keep an eye on the battens to make sure none of them catch on a shroud. Also, if your mainsheet system is attached, make sure it has plenty of slack and is not caught under a corner casting or some other piece of gear. A caught mainsheet can result in an early capsize in gusty conditions.

7. After you have raised the main all the way, the halyard must be locked off on the halyard catch at the top of the mast. Halyard catches vary, but most lock aloft at the masthead. Hold the halyard away from the mast, then bring it in until the small metal ball on the halyard catches under the U-shaped fitting on the mast (figures 21 A & B). To make sure the halyard is locked, pull down on the downhaul. Pulling on the downhaul should only remove wrinkles in the sail. If the sail moves down when you pull the downhaul the halyard isn't locked.

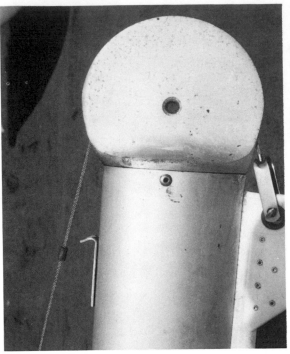

Figure 21A   Figure 21B

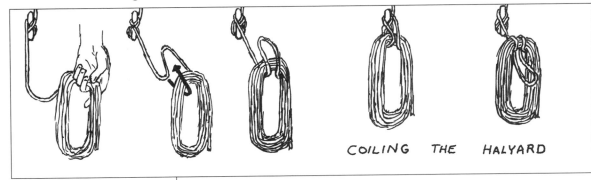

COILING   THE   HALYARD

Figure 22

8. Coil the halyard line and hang it from a cleat on the mast (figure 22).

9. Insert the gooseneck into the mast and set the downhaul (figure 23). The downhaul line should be pulled taut just enough to remove major wrinkles in the sail that develop when the sail is sheeted tightly. Once the downhaul has the correct tension, cleat it off (figure 24).

10. Attach the mainsheet ratchet block to the traveler car. The block attaches with a pin and ring set (figure 25). Then, thread the traveler and tie a figure-8 knot in the end of the mainsheet ends. Also, tie a knot in the end

LEARNING THE BASICS

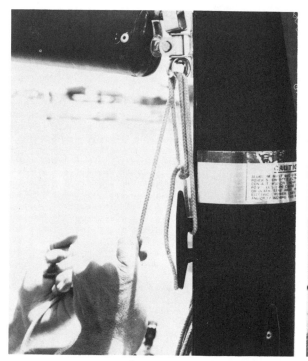

Figure 23

Figure 24

Figure 25

of the mainsheet (see Knots). If the sheet on your traveler system is "endless," then you don't need the knots.

HOISTING THE JIB

1. Attach the tack of the jib to the bridle adjuster with a shackle or pin (figure 26).
2. Attach the jib halyard to the head of the jib and secure the luff hank by twisting it onto the forestay (figure 27).
3. Secure the jibsheets to the clew of the jib (figure 28).

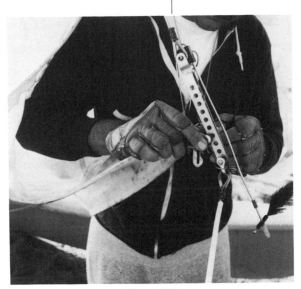

Figure 26

Figure 27

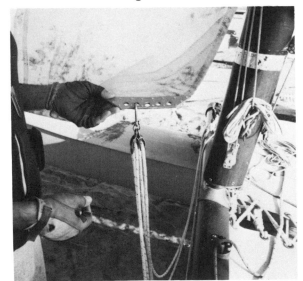

Figure 28

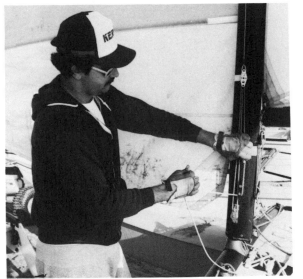

Figure 29

LEARNING THE BASICS

4. Hoist the jib with the halyard. Many cats, like the Hobie 16, let the aft load of the mast rest on the jib luff wire instead of the forestay. The thing to remember with this kind of rig is to give the halyard enough tension so the forestay is slack when the cat is sailing (figure 29). On cats where the jib rests on the forestay, jib halyard tension should be set to the point where the wrinkles disappear from the sail.

LOAD GEAR

After you've got the sails up it's time to load up your cat. Things you need are life jackets, a small paddle, righting line, extra shackles, and a ditty bag for food and personal goodies. Remember to bring clothes for the weather. If it's going to get cold later in the day, consider a wetsuit or jacket. Whatever you bring aboard, make sure it's secured tightly to the trampoline or stowed away in a storage port.

RIGGING CHECK LIST

1. Untangle the trapeze wires. Also check the shock cords and rope for wear.
2. Tape all split rings on the shrouds and forestay once you're satisfied with the pin positions. Shroud adjuster covers will work fine in lieu of tape.
3. Cover or smooth out all sharp points on board. Grey duct tape comes in handy here.
4. Tighten all shackles, screws and bolts where necessary.
5. Check the entire rudder assembly. Pins, gudgeons, tiller, rudder lock system and crossbar connectors.
6. Check the drain plugs on the sterns. Be sure they are in and sealed well before launching.
7. Snug up trampoline lacing if it needs it.
8. Make sure you have a righting line in place whenever you go sailing.
9. Check your tell-tales and masthead or bridle fly for unrestricted movement.

7/
GETTING UNDERWAY AND RETURNING TO SHORE

In the previous chapters we've gone over the basics of catamaran sailing and how to rig your cat. Now, with a light breeze, knowledge of a few right-of-way rules, and some courage, it's time to go sailing.

When you're first getting acquainted with your cat, it's a good idea to avoid strong winds and surf. Pushing off into surf or heavy winds without first mastering your cat in less demanding conditions is asking for trouble.

BASIC RIGHT-OF-WAY RULES

The rules of ocean travel are complex and vast for ocean going vessels. The rules for the racing sailor are pretty complex also, but most of them come out of common sense. The most important thing to do is yield when you're not sure of the rules. And remember, there have been plenty of sailors who went for a swim even though they had the right-of-way but stubbornly held their course when common sense dictated otherwise. Below are five important rules to know on the water. More rules are covered in chapter 12.

1. *Starboard tack.* This is the golden rule—starboard tack has the right of way over a boat on port tack. When the wind is blowing over the starboard side of your

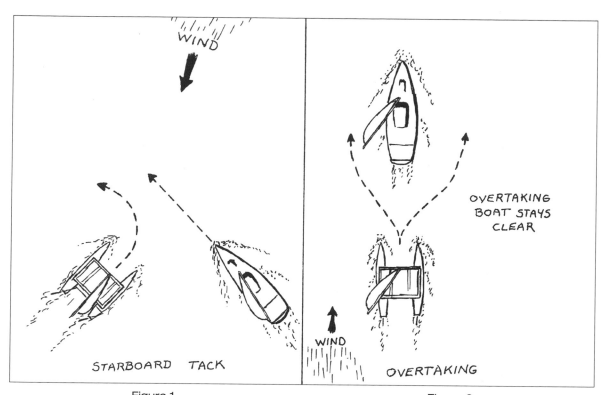

WIND

STARBOARD TACK

Figure 1

OVERTAKING BOAT STAYS CLEAR

WIND

OVERTAKING

Figure 2

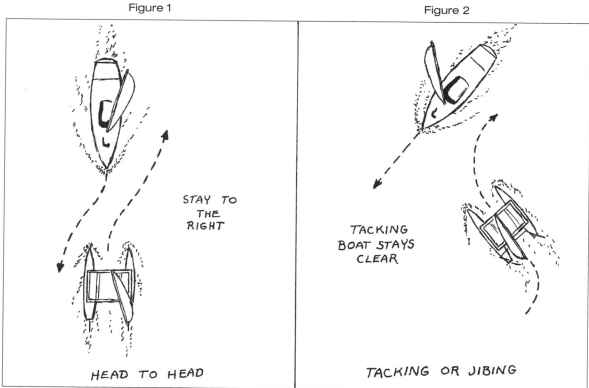

STAY TO THE RIGHT

HEAD TO HEAD

Figure 3

TACKING BOAT STAYS CLEAR

TACKING OR JIBING

Figure 4

GETTING UNDERWAY
AND RETURNING
TO SHORE

cat, you are on a star-board tack. The boat on port tack must stay clear (figure 1).

2. *Overtaking.* A boat coming up from the rear must stay clear of the boat ahead. You can pass another boat on either side, just be sure to give the boat you are passing plenty of room (figure 2).

3. *Head to head.* When two boats are approaching each other head-on, each boat must stay to the right (figure 3).

4. *Tacking or jibing.* A boat in the process of a tack or jibe must stay clear of boats that are not tacking or jibing (figure 4).

5. *Give way to larger vessels.* If you're out sailing in the harbor and a 100-foot motoryacht is heading up the channel, give it plenty of room. This only makes sense since the motoryacht is difficult to maneuver in a restricted area. The "power gives way to sail" rule does not apply where there is a great difference in size and maneuverability.

THE BRAKES

Many beginning sailors are wary of the fact that sailboats don't have brakes. While you should be conscious of this, you should also know that a catamaran can stop very quickly. All it takes is pushing the tiller away from you and letting the sail(s) out at the same time. If you find yourself heading for the world's most expensive motoryacht and you're not quite sure what to do, just shove that tiller and let your sheet(s) out. Experiment with this technique a few times and you'll discover your cat has brakes after all.

GETTING UNDERWAY

Techniques for getting underway vary depending on the area you're leaving from, weather conditions, and your skill. But using common sense will get you safely to and from the beach or landing once you have the basics down.

LAUNCHING AT A RAMP

Many cats are put into the water via a ramp or slipway. An easy way to get into trouble here is to hoist the sails before the boat is in the water. The wind is seldom blowing from the right direction, and if it's windy enough, your cat might begin flying a hull right on the trailer! But, if you launch with your sails down, make sure they are ready to go up in a hurry since most ramps don 't have enough docking space for leisurely rigging.

Before going down the ramp it's a good idea to move your cat forward on the trailer to increase weight on the tongue. This helps keep your cat securely on the trailer as it angles down the ramp. Some skippers go one step further and tie a line around the forestay and the mast support (on the trailer) to insure their cat doesn't leave the trailer prematurely.

Depending upon your chutzpah or your car, you can either walk or drive your cat down the ramp to the water. Just make

Figure 5

Figure 6

Figure 7

GETTING UNDERWAY
AND RETURNING
TO SHORE

sure the drain plugs are in! And, keep an eye on your hulls; sometimes they get a little too close to the pavement.

Back the trailer into the water until its rear end is over the water. If you can avoid getting the trailer's wheel bearings wet and still launch your cat, so much the better (figure 5).

Once you have the cat and trailer just over the water, lift the bows and roll the cat off the trailer and into the water (figure 6). Be courteous to your fellow trailer-sailors and leave your unloaded trailer in a spot where it won't interfere with other launchings. And whatever you do, leave your trailer above the high tide mark—otherwise you might have a hard time finding it when you sail back to the ramp!

When your cat is finally in the water, someone will have to hold onto it while the trailer and car are parked and the sails are hoisted. Do this by holding the cat by its painter or bridle wires so the bows will swing into the wind (figure 7).

If the wind is blowing towards the shore, you might have to wade out too far in order to hold the cat into the wind. The solution (if you want to stay dry) is to hold your cat by one of its hulls instead of the bridle wire.

LEAVING A BEACH OR RAMP

Figure 8

Leaving a beach or a ramp involves the same tactics once your boat is in the water. The only difference between ramp and

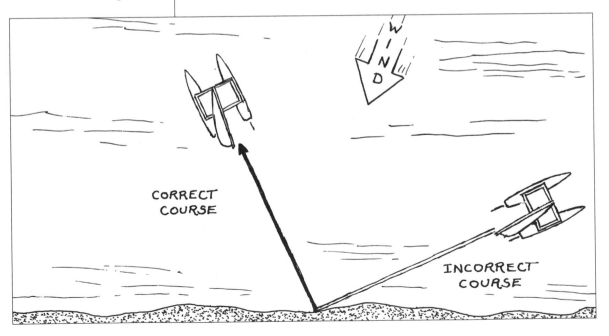

beach launching is getting to the water's edge. At a beach, a cat is either dragged, carried or rolled on beach wheels to the water. When you're ready to go sailing do the following:

1. Check out the wind direction and figure which tack will take you farther away from the beach. Almost always, one tack is much more favored than the other for getting away from the beach (figure 8).

2. Turn your cat onto the right tack and set the tiller on the proper side. Then set your traveler for the point of sail you will be on. If you're going to be beating, set it in the center, for close reaching, mid-way out, and for reaching and running, set it all the way outboard (figure 9). Note: the cat in this photo doesn't have its tiller on the correct side.

Figure 9

Figure 10

Figure 11

GETTING UNDERWAY
AND RETURNING
TO SHORE

3. Now, when you're ready, give yourself a good shove off the beach (figure 10).
4. When you're out far enough, put the rudders (and center-boards, if you have them) down and trim the sails (figure 11).
5. Remember, going through the surf with no previous experience is inviting disaster. Go sailing a few times first and read chapter 14.

The important thing to remember when leaving a dock is having your rudders and centerboards (if appropriate) down.

Figure 12

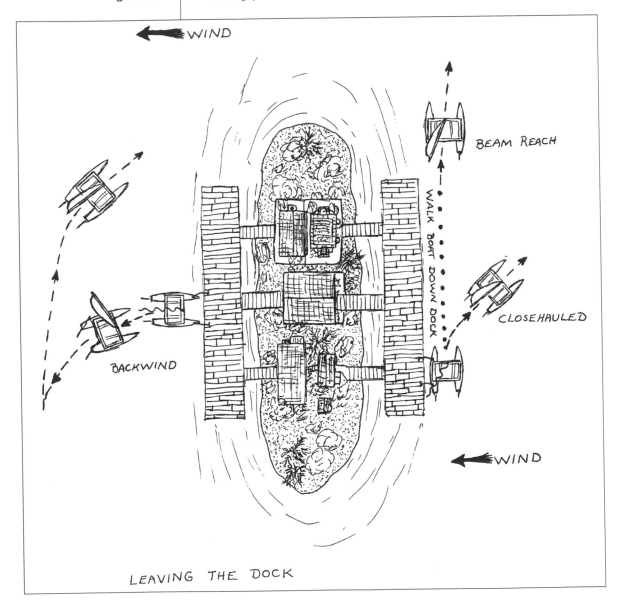

LEAVING THE DOCK

Never leave a dock until you do this, otherwise you'll have no control over your cat.

If the wind is blowing into the dock and across the beam of your cat, getting underway will take a little more effort than normal. You will have to push off the dock hard (with the traveler centered) and sheet in quickly or walk the cat down the dock (figure 12 right).

When the wind is blowing across the dock directly at your cat, either walk it to the end of the dock and shove off or back away. A windward dock is also the best one to land at because you are headed into the wind when you land. While you may have to tempt fate by walking along a bow to hop on the dock, your chances of capsizing or scratching the hulls are reduced (figure 12 left).

RETURNING TO SHORE

Landing on a beach is easy, most of the time. Just remember to raise your rudders up (if they don't kick up automatically). If you have centerboards, make sure they're up also. After sailing up on the beach, turn your cat so it's facing into the wind. Be sure you have a good place to land. If you are pulling up to a concrete ramp or a rocky beach, it's best to get off your cat in shallow water and guide it in slowly.

When approaching a beach, going slow is the key to a safe landing. Try to judge when to ease your sails out so you will glide up on the shore with a minimum of speed left. Even though a cat stops pretty fast when you turn or let the sails out, it certainly won't happen immediately. If you find yourself going too slow (which is much better than going too fast) just pull the sails in a little.

DOCKING

Docking takes more skill than beaching because you cannot run up on a dock as you can on a beach. Judging your speed and distance is much more important when you're approaching a dock. Unless you can drop your sails, avoid docking with the wind behind you. Backwinding into a dock is the least desirable method of docking (figure 13 center). Docking while on a reach is also tough, since slowing your cat down will be difficult. Always try to dock heading into the wind. But have your

Figure 13

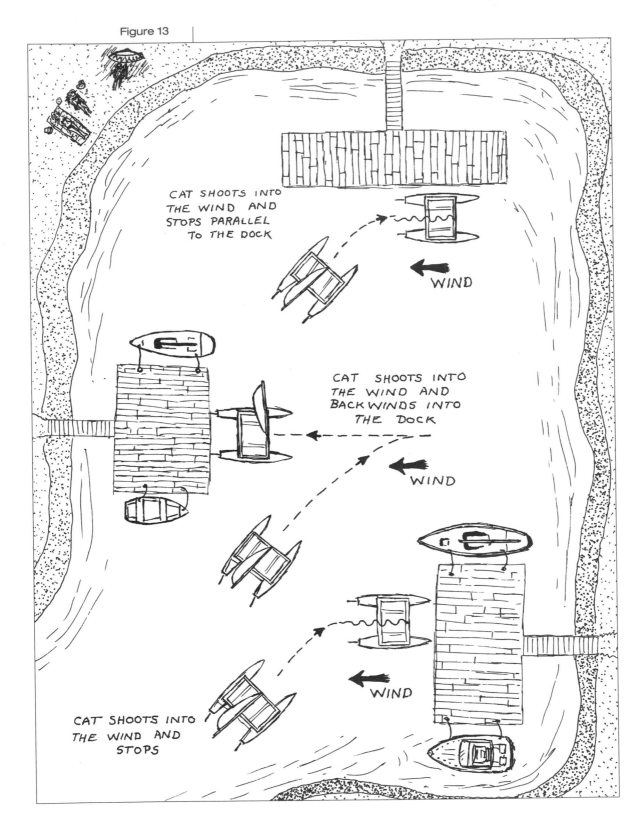

CAT SHOOTS INTO THE WIND AND STOPS PARALLEL TO THE DOCK

WIND

CAT SHOOTS INTO THE WIND AND BACKWINDS INTO THE DOCK

WIND

CAT SHOOTS INTO THE WIND AND STOPS

WIND

timing down; you want to coast up to the dock with just enough speed to get you there but no more than that (figure 13 bottom). If you have a crew, he or she should shimmy out on a bow and grab the dock before you start going backwards. If you 're alone...well, you can see it's a neat trick. If the wind is blowing parallel to the dock, just sail along and then shoot into the wind along side the dock (figure 13 top).

Try docking repeatedly on a light air day if you're new to it. The practice will give you confidence to land anywhere (and the smarts to know where not to land). Keep these tips in mind:

1. Always rig and unrig heading into the wind.
2. Try to land to leeward of any dock.
3. Make a game plan in advance for landing.
4. Remember how to use your brakes: sheet out and make a quick turn into the wind.
5. If you land downwind, take your sails down and glide into the dock. If you back in, take them down as soon as you land.
6. Don't force in on an overcrowded dock. It's much safer to sail around and wait for enough space to open up for an easy landing.

For best speed, this is about as high off the water as you'll ever want to sail upwind.

GETTING UNDERWAY
AND RETURNING
TO SHORE

UNRIGGING

Once you're back at the dock or beach after a full day of sun and sailing, you'll be in a hurry to put your cat away. Here's how to do it, starting with the mainsail, which should come down first.

1. Loosen the downhaul line completely.
2. Lift the boom and gooseneck out of the mast.
3. Remove the halyard from the mast and, with a flick of the wrist, unlock the halyard catch at the top of the mast (chapter 6).
4. Lower the halyard with one hand and pull the luff rope out of the mast with the other.
5. Unscrew the halyard shackle from the mainsail headboard and secure the shackle to a cleat (figure 14). Another good place for the shackle is inside the opening for the mast groove (figure 15).
6. Secure the mainsheet system to the boom by tying the downhaul line to the mainsheet ratchet block (figure 16).
7. Take the head of the mainsail and fold it over at the top batten. Then, roll up the sail and pull out any wrinkles that develop near the luff rope and leech (figure 17).

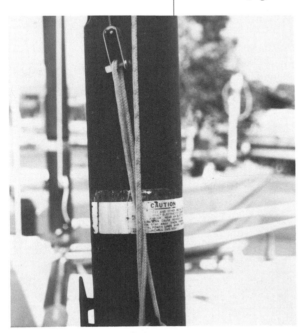

Figure 14

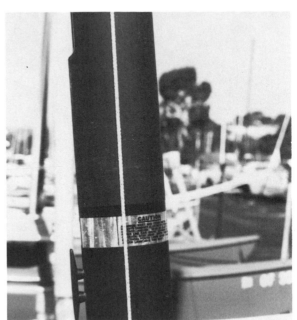

Figure 15

8. The mainsheet is fine for tying the sail up. Make sure you cover the sail and store it in a dry place.

The jib is taken down like the main unless it doesn't have battens. A jib without battens should be folded instead of rolled. Some cat sailors like to roll up their jib and stuff it into the last few rolls of the main (figure 18).

When the sails are put away, secure the rest of your cat. Tie the rudders up so they won't drop and remove the centerboards (if you have them). Cleat off the halyards snugly. It's also a good idea to stiffen up the whole mast by pulling in the jib sheets or tightening down the mast raker.

Figure 16

Figure 17

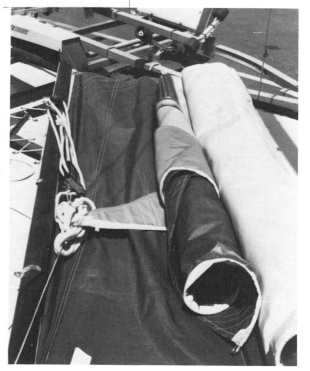

Figure 18

GETTING UNDERWAY
AND RETURNING
TO SHORE

8/
HEAVY WEATHER SAILING

While you should begin your cat sailing in lighter winds, sooner or later you'll be out in a good solid breeze, maybe even more than that. There's no way to gain confidence in your heavy air sailing abilities short of actual experience.

If you're leery of sailing in a lot of wind, try to imagine the worst that could happen—if you exercise common sense. It's usually one of three things: a capsize, dismasting, or falling overboard. If you keep your wits about you, you can recover from all of these situations.

Righting a capsized cat is fairly easy when you have done it a few times. Sooner or later you will capsize accidentally, so the best way to ease your mind about going over is to practice righting your cat on a nice light air day. You can also practice recovering a man overboard by tossing a cushion into the water and sailing up to it repeatedly. For solo sailors, it pays to be a good swimmer. Whatever your situation you should always wear a flotation device of some kind when sailing offshore.

Practicing a dismasting isn't a good idea, but you should have an idea of what to do if your mast goes over the side.

DISMASTING

If your mast comes down, try to recover everything with a minimum of damage. Things you want to avoid are broken battens and ripped sails. First, uncleat the sheets, this frees up the clews of the sails and takes strain off the mast. Once this is done, you should be able to get the mast on board. If you can't, check to see what might be catching—sometimes a shroud or the forestay has to be disconnected before the mast can be brought aboard. Getting the mast out of the water as soon as possible reduces the chances of something being broken or torn.

Once the mast is on board and lying across the middle of the cat with the top pointed forward, get the sails off quickly, especially if conditions are rough and you're going to be towed. Taking the sails off the rig involves some work. First, undo the downhaul and slide the mast toward the stern so you can reach the main halyard lock and free it. Then, pull the main off the mast and wrap it around the boom. The jib comes off more easily, except for moving out on one of the bows to undo the tack shackle.

When the sails are off, secure the mast with some line and prepare for a tow (if you should be so fortunate). Take the righting line and tie it around the middle of the front crossbar. Then sit and be ready to toss it to a good Samaritan.

If you get dismasted away from help, it means some paddling or re-stepping the mast. Re-stepping the mast in choppy water is an almost impossible task. Even in smooth water, it's

HEAVY WEATHER
SAILING

difficult to keep the mast balanced as you try to raise it. And whatever caused the dismasting (like a broken shroud) will have to be jury-rigged before you attempt to get sailing again. Most of the time, it's a matter of waiting for help. You should have a mirror on board for signaling, and hopefully you brought along some warm clothing.

MAN OVERBOARD

If your crew goes over the side, the first thing to do is throw him or her a flotation device. Usually it's a cushion or a life-jacket. Whatever it is, make sure it's not tied to the boat! If you're sailing upwind, jibe your cat as soon as possible, harden up to a reach and shoot into the wind toward the man over-board (figure A). Jibing is still the best thing to do if your crew falls over during a reach. If you're on a run, the only thing to do is harden up towards the wind, sail-closehauled, then tack for your crew member (figure B).

An overboard situation is much more serious if you fall over and your crew isn't a good sailor. It's a good idea to talk about picking up a man overboard with your crew before you go sailing. In either case, if you fall over leaving an inexperi-enced crewman on board, be prepared to yell some instruc-tions, i.e.: "Push the tiller away from you!" or, "Let the sails out!" If things look pretty bleak for your recovery, the best

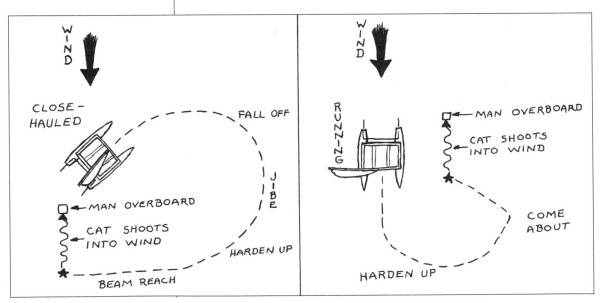

Figure A   Figure B

LEARNING THE BASICS

thing to do is have your crew capsize the cat before it takes him over the horizon. By pulling in the sheets tight, sitting on the lee side and pushing the helm away from his body, your crew should be able to flip the cat. During all of this action try to keep calm. After the cat has capsized, take your time swimming towards it—it won't go anywhere. Also, tell your crew to stay on board. You don't need two people overboard!

If you're sailing alone and go overboard, you are usually o.k.—your cat should naturally head into the wind and stop if the helm was set correctly before you went over (chapter 11). Whatever, it's a good idea to swim like hell to catch your cat before it gets a streak of independence. If the helm gets caught or you're a poor swimmer, you've got problems. Keep calm and conserve your strength. Watching your cat sail away from you while you 're treading water is no fun, but you've got to keep your wits about you to maximize your chances of being rescued.

This large C-class catamaran has its mainsail reefed for a very, very stiff breeze!

RIGHTING THE CAPSIZED CAT

Capsizing is like a first date—it's a little scary, but you almost always recover. Here are a few tips for recovering from a capsize:

1. Cardinal rule of capsizing: always hang onto your boat. Don't leave it for any reason.
2. Uncleat the sails so they won't hold any water during the righting process.
3. Untie the righting line from the leeward side. If you don't have a righting line you'll have to use the mainsheet.
4. Standing on the leeward hull, hang onto the righting line and lean outboard as far as possible (figure 1). The righting line will make balancing your weight a lot easier. The whole operation should be done with your cat floating crossways to the wind. If you're doing it right, your cat's windward hull should slowly rise (figure 2).
5. Once you've got your cat from the upside down (turtled) position to the 90-degree (capsize) position, remember you've got to keep the mast pointing towards the wind for successful righting. If you have drifted around, swim the bows back around so the mast is pointing into the wind again. Then, continue standing on the hull and leaning out with the righting line. This is the toughest part since you've got to pull the mast and sails out of the water with just your weight (figure 3).
6. As the cat comes over, hang on to the submerged (and soon to be windward) hull. By keeping your weight on the hull you'll keep your cat from flipping over again in the opposite direction. Also, watch your head as your cat finally comes back on its feet (figure 4).
7. As soon as you can, get aboard the cat and straighten things up. Look to the sheets first to make sure they won't jam and cause another capsize. After checking for any damage to the sails, you're ready to go again.

If you're on the lighter side or your mast has filled with water because of improper sealing, you might need some out side help in righting. While volunteer help means well, make sure you 're in charge during the righting operation unless your rescuers know more than you do. If a swimmer or your crew are helping you out, the biggest problem will be for both of you to keep your weight in the right place while standing on the submerged hull. Four hands on a single righting line can also be a challenge. Be patient and you'll work it out (figure 5).

If help comes in the form of a powerboat, there are a couple of ways to use it. If you're just capsized, the powerboat can

Figure 5

go to the end of the mast and someone on board can lift the mast out of the water. This will really help. But beware of the inexperienced powerboat operator—more than one cat sailor has had his sails run over by a well-meaning rescuer!

If your cat won't rise from a turtled (upside down) position despite all your efforts, attach a line (at least 25 feet long) to the forward windward crossbar and toss it to your helpers in the powerboat. Very slowly, the powerboat should pull your cat away from the wind. While this is an almost sure way of getting your cat right side up, it's also potentially dangerous if the guy in the powerboat doesn't understand the importance of going slowly when pulling the line. Make sure he understands this. If you hear cracking or groaning sounds during the operation, yell for the powerboat to stop. The sounds probably mean you have water in your hulls. If this is the case, the safest thing you can do is take your mast off and tow your cat slowly to a beach where you can check the problem out.

TRAPEZING

Trapezes have two great benefits: They're really exciting and they enable you to harness more of the wind's power for more speed.

You've got to be a pretty good sailor to use a trapeze effectively and safely. Agility on the part of the trapezer is also essential, especially in gusty conditions. Start your trapeze sailing in lighter winds and gradually work towards mastering the technique before blasting out in heavy winds all hooked in. On a two-person cat team work is the key to successful trapezing. When you're hanging out on that wire you really want to know what the boat is going to do next!

The first step in trapezing is to choose a system and harness. There are three major harness styles available today, the half-fit (or butt-bucket), the full fit, and the full-fit combo life jacket. Butt-buckets are great for upper body movement, but they don't support your back at all (figure 6). If you have a bad back or think you'll be hanging out for long periods of time,

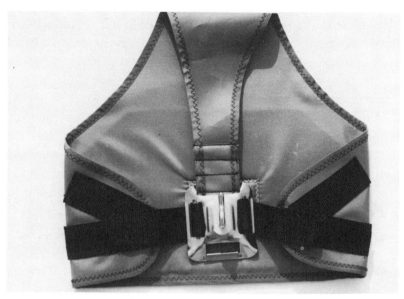

Figure 6

Figure 7

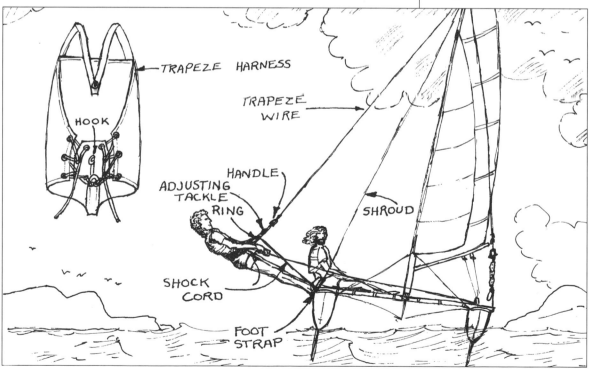

the butt-bucket isn't a good choice. Full-fit harnesses give great back support but restrict your mobility somewhat. Full-fits are also a little uncomfortable when you're not out on the wire (figure 7). The full-fit combo life jacket is the best idea, but existing models are inferior in quality compared to the standard full-fits now marketed.

Trapeze harnesses are either laced or strapped up for fit. The lace-up harness usually gives a better fit but requires more time to get into and adjust. While the strap-up doesn't fit as well as the "lacer-upper," it is much easier to use.

Trapeze wire rigs differ throughout classes of cats, but two basic types exist and both are good. The "snap-back ring set" has an adjustable band that allows the trapezer to set harness height at a single position (figure 8). The "adjusting-tackle ring set" goes a step further, allowing you to adjust your harness height while you're trapezing (figure 9). On a reach for instance, you want your body lower than you do when going to windward. But there are no hard and fast rules for height set-

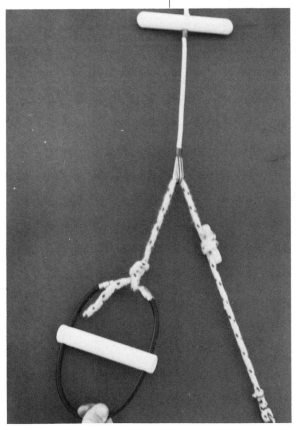

Figure 8

Figure 9

tings. Some sailors like to be higher off the water than others. Generally, you want your body lowered until you can just see down the deck or trampoline while you're fully extended. Figure 7 shows a good trapezing height.

First-time trapezers should try it while the cat is still on the beach. Have someone offset the extended weight by sitting on the opposite side. Practice adjusting height and coming in and going out on the wire. The basics of trapezing are as follows (refer to figure 10):

1. Start by sitting on the hull or sidebar with the trapeze ring hooked into the harness. On most harnesses, the hook faces down. Another rig is a new "no hook" sys-

These sailors show excellent trapeze form.

Figure 10

tem. This is a much safer system than most others because there is no danger of something catching onto your hook in a capsize.

2. Using one hand to steady yourself, slowly ease your weight over the side by pushing back on the deck or trampoline with your feet. Your other hand should be holding onto the trapeze handle for balance. Sit with your legs bent and feet on the deck or trampoline with most of your weight hanging from the wire.

3. Slip your feet out on the sidebar or hull and push yourself out over the water. When pushing, try to keep more weight on your forward foot.

4. Extend your legs and you're out. Keep your feet spread about two feet apart on the crossbar and keep your aft leg slightly bent. For coming in, reverse the entire process.

BALANCING YOUR CAT FROM A TRAPEZE

The key to balancing your cat while trapezing is to watch the hulls. If the bows begin to bury, the trapezer should move aft. If the sterns are dragging, move forward. When double-trapezing the skipper and crew should be as close together as possible. Weight centralization is what you're after. Keeping the weight close together and in the middle keeps the pitching moment of the hulls to a minimum. If you begin to fly a hull, you want all the weight out on the wire(s). The optimum angle for hull flying is just where the windward hull is skimming the water. If your weight isn't enough to keep your cat down, either ease the sheet(s) (in a gust) or set the traveler(s) or barber-haulers outboard, which spills wind from the sails (chapter 9). On the other end of the spectrum, you don't want too much weight out on the trapeze in lighter winds. While trapezing may be fun, it's slowing you down if it's causing your cat to heel to windward.

Keeping your back leg bent and your forward leg straight is essential when you're trapezing. Your bent leg acts as a shock absorber and your straight front leg is a preventer. When rapidly accelerating or climbing a swell, you bend your back leg and when dropping down a wave or suddenly slowing, you put pressure on your front leg. These constant adjustments make for faster and safer sailing.

HIKING OUT ON THE STRAPS

If you're sailing a small unarig like a Hobie 14, you hike out with the aid of straps instead of using a trapeze. The straps run fore and aft on each side of the trampoline. To hike, put your feet under the straps and hang your butt over the rail. If the leeward bow starts to bury, shift your weight aft. The more wind you sail in, the further aft your weight should be. Keeping your butt over the rail is tough work, but it really helps you sail fast in heavier air.

SAFE SAILING IN HEAVY AIR

Once you have mastered heavy air sailing there's not much else to worry about. You'll be confident that you can handle a sudden squall, make your way to shore if a strong offshore springs up, or run towards a beach in a heavy onshore wind without capsizing end-over-end. But it's catch 22; to gain such confidence you've got to go sailing when it's really blowing. Here are some tips to remember when that day comes:

BEATING IN A BLOW

Cardinal rule: Never cleat your sails. When it's howling, a sudden puff can come through so fast you won 't have time to uncleat before you capsize. It's more work, but hang on to that sheet when you're in heavy air. If you get hit with a severe blast, let the sheet out and round up towards the wind slightly. When the gust subsides, fall off again and sheet in. You can't work your cat upwind effectively unless you sail this way.

While hiking out or trapezing helps keep your cat down, if it gets really rough and gusty, it's much safer to give up a little speed and sit on the weather rail with your feet under the straps.

Another heavy air upwind technique is to ease your traveler down about 12 inches from centerline. This keeps your heel down and makes for better heavy—air sail shape. The more breeze you have, the more you should ease the traveler down. But remember that the further down the traveler is from centerline, the less pointing ability you'll have.

If you find yourself exhausted while trying to beat towards shore in an offshore wind, capsizing your cat and sitting on top of it is often the best thing to do. A capsized cat makes a good platform to rest on and it will blow out to sea slower than if it is right side up.

FORCE	WIND SPEED IN KNOTS	DESCRIPTION	SAILING CONDITIONS
0	0	Flat calm. Surface like a mirror	Sailing cats make no progress
1	1–3	Small ripples on the surface. Wind can be felt on the face	Sailing cats make slow progress and do not heel. Helmsman and Crew sit on opposite sides
2	4–6	Surface still calm, but small waves begin to form. Leaves move in the wind	Good conditions for the beginner. Cats move faster and begin to heel
3	7–10	Small waves. Crests break occasionally. Wavelets on inland waters. Branches in leaf begin to sway	Excellent sailing conditions. Some hiking-out required
4	11–16	Medium waves. Crests break fairly regularly. Waves form on inland waters	Exciting conditions for the more experienced. Most cats fly hulls
5	17–21	Larger waves. Crests break frequently. Sea becoming rough. Some breaking waves even on inland waters	Testing conditions even for the experienced cat sailor. Not recommended for beginners
6	22–27	Large waves with white breaking crests. Sea rough. Waves break regularly on open waters inland	Only suitable for expert sailors. Cats can only be kept upright by traveling the mainsail way out
7	28–33	Open sea becoming very rough. Breaking waves even in enclosed waters	Trying conditions for most cats

Weather Chart

RUNNING IN A BLOW

Keep your weight far aft when you're running in a lot of wind. Keeping your bows up is essential if you want to avoid a violent "pitch pole" capsize. If your weight is all the way aft and your bows still want to dig in, you should sail on a higher course and luff your sails a little.

Depending on the kind of rig you have and how far from shore you are, you might want to drop your sail(s). A Hobie 14 under its mast alone will do eight knots in a 45 knot tail wind. On a sloop—rigged cat you might take down the main or the jib, depending on the situation.

If you must change tacks in a blow, do it by tacking, not jibing. Jibing in heavy air is asking for a swim.

HEAVY AIR TACKING

You can't point very high in a heavy wind, and this makes tacking difficult. As soon as you turn into the wind, you'll come to a quick stop. So, when the wind is howling, nine times out of ten you'll have to do a backwind tack. Here's how to do it:

1. Be moving as fast as possible and have your traveler no more than halfway down when you begin your tack.
2. As you turn into the wind, move your weight forward. Otherwise, the wind may catch under your trampoline or deck and flip you over backwards.
3. Sheet out on your main at least one foot when you're head-to-wind. This helps the mast to rotate and the sail to fill on the new tack.
4. Backwind your main until you are sure you're through the eye of the wind. It's better to backwind too much than end up in irons when it's really blowing.

PART II
MASTERING THE FINE POINTS

9/
INTERMEDIATE SAIL HANDLING

Like any other sport, sailing becomes more rewarding after you've mastered the basics. In the previous chapters, we've gone over the minimum you need to know for that first sail in your cat. But if you really want to enjoy sailing you've got to explore the finer points of handling and tuning your cat.

To move towards sailing's finer points, start at the beginning—understanding the wind. One of the toughest things for

Figure 1

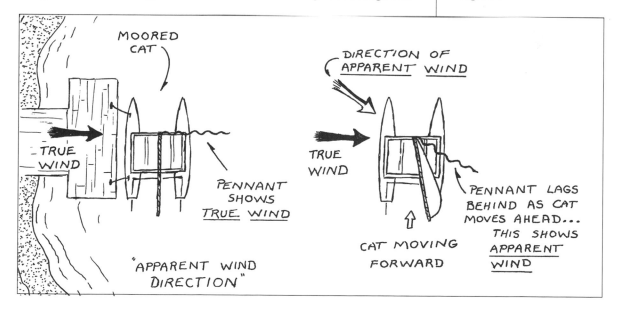

the beginning sailor to figure out is where the wind is coming from. Tell-tales, masthead flys, and bridle vanes are used by all sailors for help in determining wind direction. But what good sailors know, and you must understand, is that while your cat is moving these indicators show the apparent wind, not the actual (or true) wind. Only when your cat is sitting on the beach or tied to a dock do these indicators show a "true wind."

Apparent wind is a combination of true wind and the wind created by your cat's forward speed. When trimming sails, you must set them to the apparent wind. As your cat increases speed masthead flys and shroud yarns will increasingly lag behind as they pass through the air. These indicators always show the wind blowing farther ahead than it actually is (figure 1).

You can understand apparent wind easier by sailing your cat closehauled in a 10-knot breeze while keeping an eye on the masthead fly. The fly will show that you are sailing nearly straight into the wind when you're actually sailing at least 40 degrees away from it. Apparent wind affects you on all points of sail and for cat sailors in particular its effect on downwind sailing is very important.

TACKING DOWNWIND

During the first half of the 19th century it was discovered that a lightweight, low frictioned boat with a high, instead of low, aspect ratio sail plan, could sail faster than the true wind was blowing (figure 2). This discovery and the sailboats it fostered greatly influenced how sailors sail downwind today.

A bulky keelboat could set a spinnaker downwind in an eight knot breeze and, if everything was going right, sail at eight knots. In the same eight knots of wind, a new "high aspect flyer" would not sail dead downwind. Instead, the skipper of such a boat would head up a little and zig-zag downwind in a series of broad reaches. By broad reaching instead of running, the wind flow on the leeward side of the sails was increased—which led to a big increase in speed. With more apparent wind, which generated more speed, the high aspect flyer sailed faster downwind than the keelboat. True, the high aspect flyer covered a lot more distance, but the increase in speed more than made up for it. Today, the key to sailing fast downwind is to head up from a run to where the most speed in relation to distance is. Simply put, a cat that tacks downwind

HIGH ASPECT RATIO

LOW ASPECT RATIO

Figure 2

Figure 3

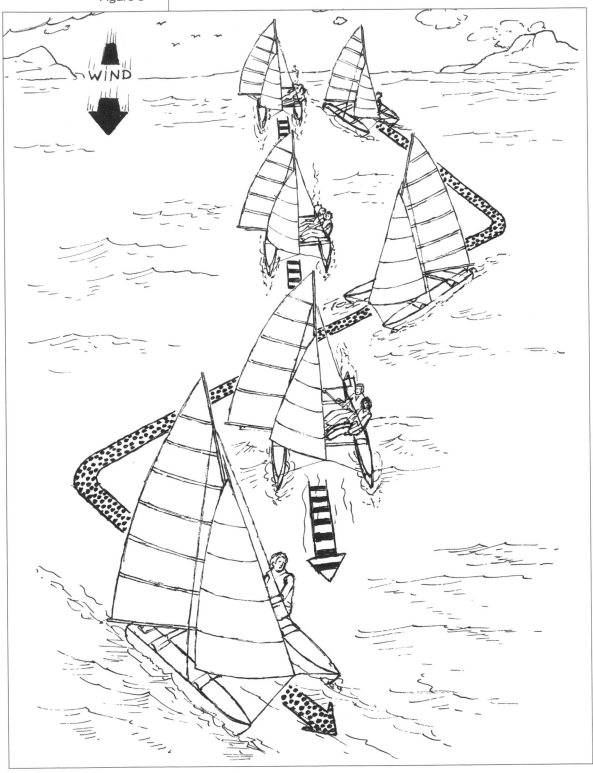

MASTERING
THE FINE POINTS

in a series of zig-zags will reach its destination sooner than a cat that runs directly before the wind (figure 3).

Good cat sailors know they should never let the back side of a sail lose the flow of wind across it. And this means never sailing directly downwind. While many top sailors know or "feel" when they are not getting a flow of wind across the back of a sail, most sailors rely on tell-tales for downwind sail trim.

TELL-TALES

Tell-tales are like American Express cards—people who sail shouldn't leave the dock without them. These ribbons and strings really help you sail because they respond to the wind long before a luff and tell you when you're oversheeted or sailing too low.

Tell-tales are simple to use. Just keep them aligned and flowing straight back across the sail. Most cats have small windows in their sails so the crew can observe the tell-tales on the leeward side of the sails (figure 4). If the leeward tell-tale begins to "break" and flutter around, the flow of air across the back-

Figure 4

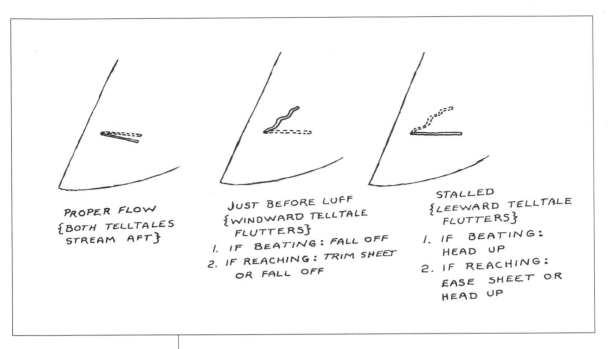

PROPER FLOW
{BOTH TELLTALES
STREAM AFT}

JUST BEFORE LUFF
{WINDWARD TELLTALE
FLUTTERS}
1. IF BEATING: FALL OFF
2. IF REACHING: TRIM SHEET
OR FALL OFF

STALLED
{LEEWARD TELLTALE
FLUTTERS}
1. IF BEATING:
HEAD UP
2. IF REACHING:
EASE SHEET OR
HEAD UP

Figure 5

side of the sail is being disrupted. When this occurs, the cat should be headed closer to the wind or the sail should be let out. The important thing is that the tell-tales should always be flowing straight back across the sails (figure 5).

When sailing upwind, your sails stay inboard, so when the leeward tell-tale goes haywire you should head up. If the windward tell-tale starts to lift, you should fall off the wind (figure 5).

Another good reason for not sailing directly downwind is that tell-tales don't work. This is because the leeward tell-tale is completely cut off from air flow and just flops around.

DOWNWIND SAIL TRIM

With an understanding of how tell-tales work, you can keep your sails working at their optimum, especially when you're tacking downwind. The course that gives the most speed for the least extra distance is about 135 degrees from the wind, or about 90 degrees from the apparent wind (figure 6).

When your shroud yarns are streaming directly across your cat, you've got a 90-degree apparent wind. If you sail higher than 90 degrees (to 70 or 80 degrees) the shroud yarns will angle forward of the beam. And if you sail too low (100 to 110 degrees off the wind) the shroud yarns will angle behind the beam. So, to keep the wind at 90 degrees, watching the

Figure 6

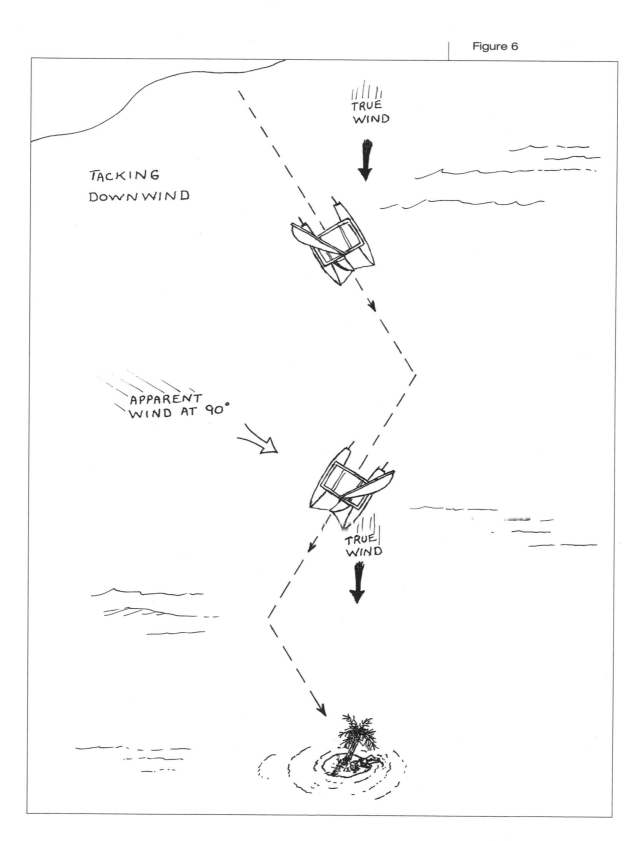

TACKING DOWNWIND

TRUE WIND

APPARENT WIND AT 90°

TRUE WIND

INTERMEDIATE SAIL
HANDLING

shroud yarns is critical. You want to sail as low on the wind as you can without cutting off the flow of air across the backside of your sail(s). A good way to get at this trim is to start the run with your sail(s), traveler(s) and/or barber hauler all the way out. From this point, slowly trim the sail(s) in and head up until the leeward tell-tale begins to lift and flow aft. If the shroud yarns don't indicate a 90-degree apparent wind, you have to either alter your course or sail trim until they do. Remember, you can't get a 90-degree apparent wind if your sails are not receiving air flow across their leeward sides.

Reaching downwind in a series of tacks is something most catamarans do with no problem. However, una-rigged cats with less than 130 square feet of sail area cannot sail effectively by tacking down wind with the wind at 90 degrees. Small una-rigs just can't generate enough speed with the wind at 90 degrees to justify the extra distance sailed.

SAIL TRIM

When the wind first strikes the luff of a sail, it splits, flowing to both its windward and leeward sides. The wind slows as it passes over the windward (concave) side of the sail, which causes pressure. On the leeward (convex) side of the sail, the wind flows much faster, causing a decrease in pressure that produces lift (figure 7). Known as the Bernoulis Principle, this lift is essential for sailing—without it, you would be unable to sail upwind. And to use this lift, cats need either centerboards or asymmetrical hulls to deter sideslip. Without boards or asymmetrical hulls, cats could only sail on broad reaches and runs.

Figure 7

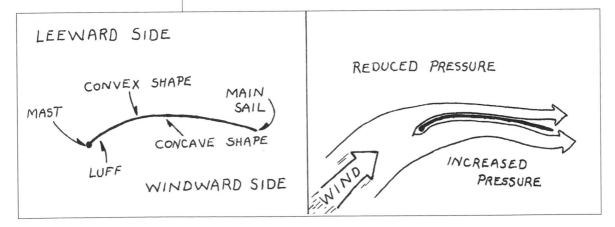

MASTERING
THE FINE POINTS

LEECH TRIM

One way to increase the aerodynamic efficiency of a sail (which leads to an increase of lift) is to keep its leech well-trimmed. The amount of curve, either to windward or leeward, in a sail's leech is a very important aspect of sail trim.

When sailing upwind with your sails sheeted in tightly, your leeches may sometimes "hook" past the centerline of your cat. Conversely, you may notice that the leeches of your sails "sag" off to leeward of centerline. A noticeable hook or sag in a leech has to be corrected because the wind will not be flowing across your sails properly. A poorly trimmed leech leads to a slower cat. A hooking leech is corrected by sheeting or traveling out (figure 8). A sagging leech is corrected by taking oppo-

Figure 8

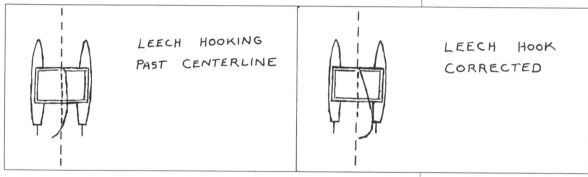

INTERMEDIATE SAIL
HANDLING

Figure 9

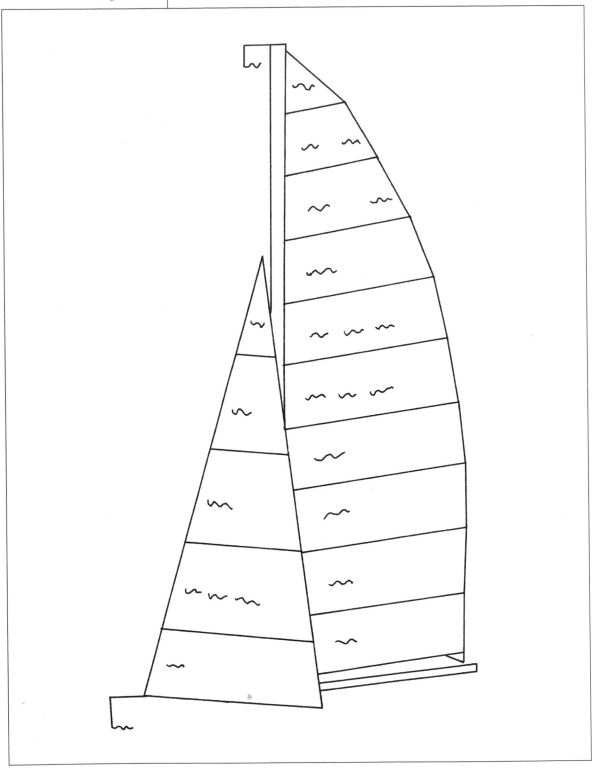

site measures. Tell-tales can help here if they are placed on the upper aft areas of the sails (figure 9). A flopping leeward tell-tale indicates a hooked leech (sheet out or travel out) and a flopping windward telltale usually means a saggy leech (sheet in or travel in). Also, remember that the more your mast bends or the wind comes up, the more your leeches will sag.

THE SLOT

If you've got a sloop-rigged cat, your jib does a lot more than just help you tack. It also greatly increases the efficiency of the main. By controlling the wind flow over the jib with good sail trimming, the convex side of the main ends up with more wind flow and reduced pressure generating more power. With sympathetic trimming of the sailplan on a sloop-rigged cat, the cat sailor gets the most from his boat.

Before setting the slot (the area between the main and the jib) it is important to have the mainsail set correctly. Once the main is trimmed, then the jib is brought in just to the point where the wind flows evenly (and therefore faster) through the slot. Figure 10A shows well-trimmed sails and a good slot between them. Pressure on the leeward side of the mainsail is reduced as the wind speed increases through the slot. In figure l0B, an "open slot" is shown; the wind's direction is not changed enough because the jib is undertrimmed—resulting in lost speed potential. Figure 10C shows a closed slot. Here the wind is forced against the leeward side of the main, causing it to luff badly. A jib that's pulled in too tight destroys the wind flow on both sides of the mainsail, greatly reducing its driving force.

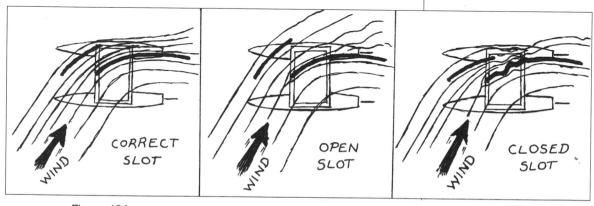

| Figure 10A | Figure 10B | Figure 10C |

INTERMEDIATE SAIL HANDLING

The perfect slot is achieved, once the main is set, by a combination of good sheet, traveler (or barber hauler) position, and a well-adjusted jib lead.

Setting goodies like jib travelers or barber haulers is easy. Just sheet in the jib tightly so the tell-tales are flowing right and the leech looks good. Then, have your crew duck down to leeward and take a look at the slot. Your crew should be watching for a slot that might be too open or closed. If the leech of the jib is hooked towards the main, it will throw air against the back of it causing it to luff. To widen the slot, the jib traveler or barber hauler should be moved to leeward. A jib leech that is too loose will hook away from the main, creating a slot that is too wide for efficient sailing. If the slot is too wide (where pulling in the sail doesn't close the slot enough without distorting its shape) the traveler or barber hauler needs to come inboard.

FAIRLEADS

Catamarans with adjustable fairleads, like the Tornado and Hobie 18, have another way to adjust the slot. With jib fairleads (blocks) that can be moved eight inches towards the bow or stern, these cats have excellent control over jib shape.

If the lead is set too far aft, the foot of the jib will be too tight and the leech too loose, since there will be more pull (from the sheet) on the foot of the sail than the leech. This creates a slot that is too open. A jib lead that is set too far forward will cause the leech of the jib to hook, which closes off the slot (see figures 10A & 10B).

Leads and travelers are constantly being adjusted by good sailors when they're sailing. In light winds and flat seas (where power is not usually needed) the mainsail can be set up flatter and can be moved more towards centerline by moving the traveler to windward. This brings the correct slot position closer amidships, which means the jib lead will probably need to be moved further aft. When you need to get maximum power from your sails (in choppy water or on reaches) you may want to increase batten tension in the main (chapter 11). This will give you a fuller and more powerful sail—but watch out, for too much batten tension will give you a hooked leech. To correct a hooked leech, ease the traveler down. If you choose to let the mainsail down to leeward with the traveler,

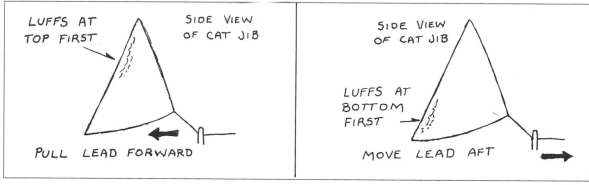

Figure 11A   Figure 11B

you'll also probably want to move the jib leads forward. Moving the leads forward will create a healthy curve in the jib, which will match the mainsail and give you the best performance for the conditions.

Tell-tales are also helpful in determining a good lead. The luff of the jib, regardless of the wind conditions, should always flow back across the sail evenly. Figure 11A shows a jib that is luffing at the head but not along the rest of the luff. This means the lead is too far aft. Figure 11B shows a bottom luff first, indicating a lead that is set too far forward.

Going another step into the possibilities of sail adjustment, you should know about clew plates. Clew plates are plastic or aluminum plates found at the clews of some cat jibs. The plates have three to eight holes in them along the outer edge, providing the same kind of adjustment that fairleads give. The holes in a clew plate allow you to attach your jib blocks high or low, depending on the cut of your sail or the conditions. If the blocks are set through a lower hole, there is reduced leech tension and more pull on the lower luff. Set higher on the clew plate, the blocks will increase leech tension. Clew plates are a good alternative to fairleads and can be easily installed.

THE TRAVELER

If you keep an eye on your mainsail as you ease the sheet and fall off to a reach, you'll see the boom rise and the top of the mainsail sag off to leeward. While the lower part of the mainsail will be set for a close reach, the top part will be set for a beam reach. This means that the sail is spilling wind, and with it lots of power. The traveler corrects this problem because it changes the angle at which your sheets pull on the sail. By letting the traveler down as you fall off you eliminate excessive sail twist (figure 12). A little sail twist isn't such a bad thing because the wind blows faster, and further behind, aloft. But if your tell-tales are not giving consistent readings from head to foot, you are traveled or sheeted incorrectly.

Remember, the traveler mainsheet relationship effects leech tension as much as luff curve. If you're on a close reach with the mainsail sheeted in too hard, (causing a hooked leech) you can get the tell-tales flowing again by pulling the traveler up a bit and easing your mainsheet. The result will be a more curved (powerful) sail and a good-looking leech. It takes working both the mainsheet and the traveler together to achieve perfect sail shape.

The traveler is also a crucial adjusting tool in heavy winds (chapter 8). If you're having trouble holding your cat down in a blow, moving the traveler out (down) will allow wind to spill. The further out the traveler goes, the more wind is spilled. While cruisers usually ease their travelers in a blow, racing sailors keep their traveler(s) in fairly close to centerline and ease their sheets in a gust. This is called keeping a *close traveler*; instead of the traveler being eased down the sheet is con-

Figure 12

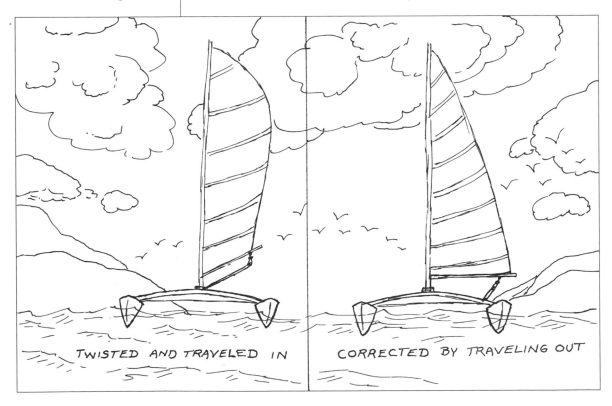

TWISTED AND TRAVELED IN   CORRECTED BY TRAVELING OUT

MASTERING
THE FINE POINTS

stantly adjusted as the wind dictates. Keeping a close traveler is tough, but it's also fast. If you are sailing with a traveler that is way out, then you're *keeping an easy traveler*; instead of working the sails so much, the traveler is let down. While having the traveler down in a gust gives good trim, the sail will usually be undertrimmed in periods of less wind.

JIB BARBER HAULERS

The jib barber hauler does the same thing as a jib traveler; it moves the jib sheet either further outboard or inboard (figure 13). This action widens and narrows the slot between the mainsail and jib. If your cat is set up with a barber hauler system, use it like a traveler—the more you fall down the sailing circle (away from the wind) the more you should pull out on the barber hauler sheet. By pulling out on the barber hauler sheet, you place the jib at a wider angle to the wind. Heading up the sailing circle (towards the wind) the barber hauler is eased, narrowing the jib's angle to the wind.

Most of the time, the main traveler is set first, and then the barber hauler is set. Basically, you want the jib to follow the set

Figure 13

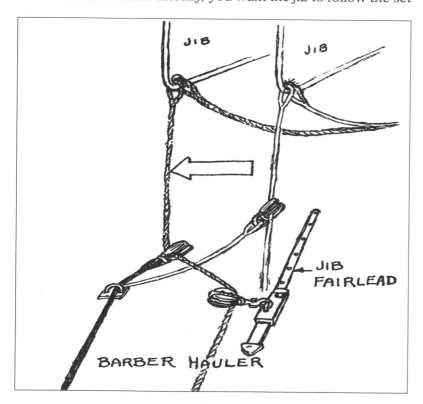

of the main since the main is a much larger sail and is most important for speed.

BOOMVANG

The boomvang is a block and tackle arrangement that runs from the underside of the boom to the base of the mast. The vang's job is similar to that of the traveler. The boomvang is more important on monohulls than it is on cats, since monohulls, with their narrow beams, have short travelers compared to cats.

On smaller una-rigs, like the Hobie 14, the boomvang comes in handy as a *preventer* since these cats must run dead downwind instead of reach when the wind is behind them. When on a run, many small-cat sailors unhook the vang from the mastbase and attach it to the front crossbar, which makes a good preventer. But whatever you do, if you've got a preventer rigged, make sure you take it off before a jibe!

The boomvang is not that important on a sloop-rigged cat because the sails must be constantly worked while off the wind. The boom vang, which cleats off, is too time consuming to work with when you're coping with wind shifts and changing wind velocity. Some cat skippers rig special vangs with a powerful shock cord. The cord, while strong enough to keep the boom from lifting a lot, still allows the skipper to sheet in and out rapidly. Even so, most sloop-rigged cats sail without the aid of boomvangs.

10/
PERFORMANCE SAIL HANDLING

In recent years you've probably seen a few catamarans sailing with huge multi-colored spinnakers, or large jibs that appear to envelope the entire cat in a sea of Dacron—or Mylar as the case may be. In the early days of catamaran sailing, from the 1950s through the 1970s, such sails were seldom seen. Only the old Pacific Catamaran, a popular boat on the West Coast, ever sailed with a spinnaker. With the advent of professional catamaran racing in the mid-1980s, however, all this changed. Top-notch racers began to see that catamarans with spinnakers and reachers moved at red-hot speed.

The only drawback with all this extra sail area is that capsizes became far more common—and a great deal more dramatic. After all, anytime you add two hundred or more extra square feet of sail area to a light catamaran it's like adding nitro fuel to a car. Things can get very touchy, especially when the wind pipes up. This said, there are several things you can do to sail safely and comfortably with big performance sails. Here, then, we explore the "how's and why's" of using spinnakers, reachers, and fathead mainsails. We'll start with the largest sail first, the spinnaker.

SPINNAKERS

Basically there are only two types of spinnakers: symmetrical and asymmetrical. Both are more affectionately known to racing sailors as "chutes."

Symmetrical spinnakers are cut like large half-balloons. They are very round and full. As you might expect, such a sail can only be used when sailing dead downwind or on very broad reaches. If you tried to take such a sail closer to the wind it would simply collapse on the front edge and blow back into the boat. For this reason very few beach cats sailed with symmetrical spinnakers. As I said earlier in chapter 9, cats go much faster tacking downwind at a 90-degree angle to the ap-

This Hobie 20 is sailing with an asymmetrical spinnaker on a pole

Nacra 6.0 with large reacher racing in the Worrell 1000 race from Ft. Lauderdale, Florida, to Virginia Beach, Virginia.

parent wind. So the only cats that use symmetrical spinnakers are heavier cruising models because they can't generate much apparent wind speed. Down in the Caribbean, for example, most of the large charter cats carry only one large symmetrical spinnaker.

Asymmetrical spinnakers are cut flat on one side and curved on the other, which makes it possible for them to be carried fairly close to the wind. Anytime the wind is hitting the boat near 130 degrees true wind you can use an asymmetrical spinnaker, provided that it isn't too windy for your abilities.

RIGGING AND HOISTING THE SPINNAKER

If you are just beginning I wouldn't suggest using your spinnaker in winds over 8 knots. As you get better you'll be able to handle higher winds. In fact, top sailors often carry spinnakers in winds up to 30 knots. But the catamaran is, of course, always on the edge when the winds are up this high—one false step with the big chute and over she goes. So start out in the light stuff, take off the stress and grow slowly.

All right, so we've got a nice sunny day and the winds are blowing between four and eight knots. Lets hit the water and hoist the spinnaker. Here are the steps:

1. First rig the spinnaker. This is done simply by attaching the spinnaker sheets to the port and starboard clews (as you would on any jib). Then clip on the spinnaker halyard to the head of the sail. Now your spinnaker is ready to be hoisted from its bag.

2. If your have a roller furling jib you need to decide if you want to roll it in or leave it out. In most cases, if you have a spinnaker pole on your cat, you will want to leave your jib up. After all, unless the conditions are very windy, you want to carry as much sail as you can when going downwind. However, if your cat has a bridle rig and not a bowsprit pole (which shortens the distance between the front of your spinnaker and the jib), roll up your jib when using the spinnaker.

3. Ultimately you will want to sail with your spinnaker at a 90-degree angle to the apparent wind, as discussed in chapter 9. But to set the spinnaker you need to head a bit lower than this so the wind is coming more from behind you, say at 120-degree angle to your windvane. Once on this course have your crew ease the jib a foot or two and have him or her cleat it off.

4. Now that you are heading downwind it is your job, as skipper, to hoist the spinnaker halyard, lifting the sail up as fast as you can, hand over hand, with the tiller resting on your lap. As you hoist the spinnaker your crew should pull the spinnaker's tack to the end of the pole. Then he should grab the spinnaker sheet and quickly pull it in when you have raised the spinnaker all the way.

5. Now, suddenly, pop, your spinnaker will fill up like a great big balloon and the cat will really take off. Try not to panic. Just stay calm and head up a little bit until the boat is sailing at a 90-degree angle to the apparent wind.

SAILING FAST WITH THE SPINNAKER

The good news about sailing downwind with an asymmetrical spinnaker is that it's a lot like tacking downwind with a jib. In fact it's almost identical. The goal is to keep wind blowing across both sides of the spinnaker. This is done very simply by attaching tell-tales to both sides of the spinnaker about 6 inches back from the luff and about 6 to 8 feet up front from the bottom of the sail. If the tell-tale on the leeward side of the spinnaker goes haywire, you are sailing too low on the wind. You must steer the boat higher. If the tell-tale on the windward side isn't flowing back properly, you are sailing too high. You must steer the boat lower. And so it goes as you play the gusts and shifts while sailing downwind.

Remember that whenever the boat really slows down it's a good bet you are sailing too low and need to head back up.

Inter 20 roaring down-wind with spinnaker. One false move, and she'll capsize.

And when you get a nice puff of wind and your apparent wind swings forward, you probably need to fall off.

As far as trimming the spinnaker is concerned, your crew should do it in much the same way he or she would trim a jib on any reach. When you start to get going really fast and the sail begins to luff, ask your crew to sheet in tighter. When the wind dies, or when your spinnaker loses contact with wind on the leeward side, ask your crew to sheet out a bit.

When the wind gets really heavy your crew won't need to do much fine trimming of the spinnaker because you will be doing almost everything with your steering. If your boat starts to fly a hull, for example, you want to head down immediately by pulling the tiller. When the puff settles down and your boat is sailing flat again, you can head back up. Be very careful here! Notice that this is the opposite way of dealing with a flying hull than when you're sailing upwind. Upwind, you head up to bring the windward hull back down. Downwind you fall off. If you head up too much in a big puff with a spinnaker, chances are you will capsize. So, remember this simple formula for sailing downwind with a spinnaker: IF IT FLIES, DRIVE OFF.

When it's really blowing one good secret to helping you drive off in the puffs is to ease the mainsheet. At this point you should have the main traveler set about a foot or two down the track, but never more than that. By easing the mainsheet you reduce healing pressure on the boat and allow the wind to push your spinnaker down naturally—and along with it the boat—rather than relying on the rudders alone. After you get the boat back down on both hulls you can begin to head back up again.

Remember, if it really gets windy and you get scared there are two things you can do. One is to sail the boat on a very low course downwind, never allowing the hull to fly. This is a much slower way to sail but a much safer approach in heavy air. The other thing you can do is drop the spinnaker. If you are racing, you probably won't follow this option, but if you aren't, it's the only sensible thing to do.

JIBING THE SPINNAKER

If you were sailing with a round symmetrical spinnaker, jibing would be a big operation because you'd have to take the spinnaker pole and move it from one side of the boat to the other.

Not so with an asymmetrical spinnaker, which is jibed just like a big jib. All you do is steer downwind and keep on turning until the boat jibes, making sure your crew uncleats the old tack of the spinnaker and hauls in on the new tack very fast as you turn through the eye of the wind. Normally, when the mainsail is crossing over the back of the back of the boat the spinnaker should also be pulled over onto the new tack. Remember, however, that if you oversteer the boat after the jibe—heading the cat up too high too fast—you run the risk of

Taking down the spinnaker before heading up wind.

Flat reaching spinnakers.

INTERMEDIATE TUNING

capsizing, especially in heavy weather. So ease up into the wind very slowly after a jibe in heavy air.

DROPPING THE SPINNAKER

When you've had enough, or need to turn around and head back upwind, you've got to drop the spinnaker. Here's how it's done:

1. Center your mainsail traveler and pre-set your mast rotation if you have a rotating mast. If you rolled up your jib, unroll it. Then have your crew sheet the jib in tight, as you would while going upwind.

2. When you are ready to drop the sail steer downwind. Now is the time for your crew to hustle down to the leeward side of the boat and grab the foot of the spinnaker. When he says he has it, you should start easing off the halyard as he gathers in the sail as it drops down. Keep an eye on what is happening. If the sail starts to get near the water, stop easing the halyard. Hold on tight until your crew safely has the spinnaker under control. When things are in hand you can start to ease the halyard again.

3. When the sail is almost down your crew needs to un-cleat the tack so that she can pull the entire spinnaker onto the trampoline and stuff in into the bag. This operation requires fast work on behalf of your crew. You can help a lot, however, by keeping your boat on a nice smooth arc and easing the halyard only when your crew has the sail under control as it is being dropped.

If all of the above stuff sounds a bit complicated, don't be too concerned. When you get out on the water it will all make perfect sense. My only recommendation is that you take it SLOWLY! After you get the hang of it, you'll be a chute meister for life.

REACHERS AND SCREECHERS

In recent years many small cat sailors have added another big sail to the front of the boat. These new larger, lighter weight jibs, are called either reachers or screechers. The reacher is normally cut from very light sailcloth and used only when reaching or running to power up the boat in light air. The screecher, a sail popularized by Olympic Tornado silver medalist Randy Smyth, is used both upwind and downwind.

Using reachers and screechers is identical to using jibs. They just happen to be a lot bigger and a little bit lighter in weight. As with all sails, you sail them with the tell tales flowing aft on both sides.

The screecher is a most interesting sail. It's generally set up on a roller furling system forward of the standard jib. In light airs it's rolled out and used to enhance performance when sailing upwind. It can generally be carried upwind in breezes up

This Hobie 21 is obviously ready to fly, with all the latest go-fasts, including a light-weight reacher called a "hooter." This somewhat lighter and fuller reacher was developed by Rick White. These custom made sails are cut by Calvert Sailmakers in Florida.

This F28 trailerable trimaran sports a large, flat-cut reacher on a furling system. Note how the boat is sailing well upwind in very light air.

to twelve knots. When the wind gets any heavier than this the screecher is rolled up. But when you start sailing downwind again the screecher can be rolled back out.

FATHEAD MAINSAILS

Most mainsails have a tear-drop shape at the top, creating a sail that looks much like a triangle. The problem is that way up at the top of the mast, where the wind blows most powerfully, you have very little sail area. One way to get around this problem is to put a square-top, or fathead, at the top of the mainsail. The advantages to this sail are twofold. First, it gives you much more sail area up high, thus generating a lot more power. Second, because the roach of the sail is so large it tends to blow off naturally in heavy air, spilling wind that would otherwise create unwanted heal. So the fathead produces a best of both worlds situation—more power in light air, less power in heavy air.

The great problem with the fathead main is that in light air

MASTERING
THE FINE POINTS

many people tend to sheet the sail in way too tightly, which causes the leech to hook to windward. This stalls the boat terribly, for the wind is unable to flow off the back of the sail smoothly. So be very careful if you have one of these sails not to sheet too tightly when sailing upwind in light air. In heavy air, the fathead has a way of taking care of itself. All you do is put a lot of pressure on the downhaul, which brings the pocket

Fathead mainsail.

of the mainsail forward. This allows the fathead leech to sag off naturally in heavy air gusts.

Spinnakers, reachers, screechers and fatheads are not for everyone. For the most part, it's the racing sailor and speed fanatic who wants these sails. But after you master the basics of cat sailing you really should try these sails. They add a new level of thrill to the sport—and isn't that what catamaran sailing is all about!

11/
INTERMEDIATE TUNING

As you acquire good sail handling skills, you should keep in mind the second (and equally important) part of getting the most from your cat—tuning. Starting with sails then working on the rudders and mast, tuning is a continuous process that allows you to get that little "extra" in speed.

Tuning a cat is similar to changing or shifting the gears on a car. As in car racing, there is both "uphill" and "downhill" sailing. Sailing through choppy seas is going uphill; you have to shift into low gear by adjusting the sails or rig. In smooth seas or when you're sailing downwind, you should shift into high gear.

Shifting "gears" for changing sea and wind conditions is what tuning is all about. Good cat sailors are constantly adding power (low gear) and reducing it (high gear). Changing gears takes a solid knowledge of all the tools available to you. Let's start with the sails.

When a sailmaker starts to design a sail for a racing cat, his primary consideration is whether he wants a sail that will enable the boat to point higher or one that will help it move faster. What he ends up with is a compromise between speed and pointing ability. When making a sail for a monohull, a sailmaker is usually more concerned with pointing, since most monohulls can't sail faster than the wave they create and can't take full advantage of apparent wind. Good monohull sails must derive a lot of lift and power from the amount of sail area available. To get this, monohull sails are cut very full (deeply curved) compared to catamaran sails.

When making cat sails, a sailmaker goes for a faster sail instead of one that is better for pointing. Since most cats attain high speeds and get a lot of help from apparent wind, sailmakers try to strike a good balance between lift and drag. Consequently, cat sails are very flat (less curve) compared to monohull sails. And while the typical monohull sail usually has the deepest part of its curve (maximum draft) in the middle, a typical cat sail has the deepest part of its curve about one-third of the way back from the sails leading edge (figure 1).

DRAFT

When sailors talk about draft or camber depth, they're speaking of a sail's convexity. A full (deeply curved) sail is capable of producing lots of lift and power. A flat sail produces less power, but also creates less drag at higher speeds; it won't luff as much because the wind can flow across it faster. Since cats are capable of reaching higher speeds than monohulls, they need flatter sails that will go through the wind faster and still be effective. How flat a sail actually is depends on many fac-

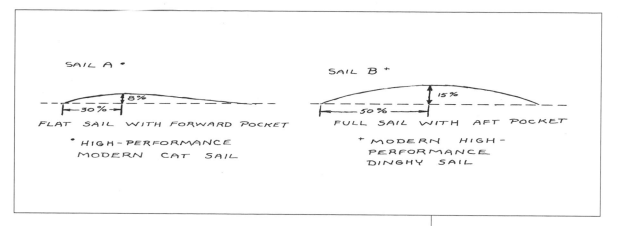

Figure 1

tors, including hull design, spar height, and overall weight. A Tornado cat, which is very light, broad beamed, and sharp hulled with a high aspect sailplan, carries a very flat sail.

POCKET

The pocket of a sail is the point where the draft is the deepest between its forward edge and the leech. The theory behind pocket position runs like this: "The more sail area that is forward of the pocket, the more lift is created for the given amount of draft." It's a little confusing, but this is why monohulls need to have the pockets of their sails farther aft than catamarans do. Cats don't need as much lift as monohulls since they are light and accelerate very quickly. A monohull-type sail on a cat would give excess lift, which usually leads to drag. Cats sail the fastest with the pocket of their sails between 30 and 40 percent aft of the sail's leading edge (figure 1).

JIB SHAPE

Since the jib is much smaller than the mainsail on a cat, it is designed to accommodate the mainsail. Sailmakers usually know what kind of mainsail needs to be cut and will cut the jib to match it. If your sails are evenly matched and tuned correctly, the tell-tales on the jib should be streaming when the tell-tales on your main are streaming. If the tell-tales on both sails are flowing but the slot between them is closed, the leech of your jib probably needs re-cutting. But before determining that you need to visit a sailmaker, be sure your cat's sails are set correctly so they will be given a good chance to perform (chapter 9).

Figure 2

BASIC SAIL TUNING

One of the best ways to begin sail tuning is to flip your cat over on a beach and take a good look at the sails (figure 2). With a stick or can propping up the mast, sheet the mainsail in tight and pull the downhaul until the major crosswrinkles in the sail disappear. Now, you can even up the pocket. If you spot irregular bulges in the sail, remove them by adjusting batten tension near the affected area. If one area is flatter than another, try tightening the batten in the flat area to induce more curve.

What you're after is a regular and smooth draft from head to foot. While the top and bottom of the sail will be flatter than the middle, what you *don't* want is an irregular change of draft from one sail panel to the next. By working with the batten tension in the sail, an even shape will emerge.

Useful tools for batten adjustment are "quick change batten tension adjusters." They can be found at your local cat shop (chapter 5).

BATTEN TENSION

During regattas, cat sailors often change the batten tension in their sails between races. Since wind and sea conditions rarely remain the same throughout the day, changing the draft of sails by messing around with the battens is important if a racer wants to remain competitive. Battens should be tightened if the seas become choppy and more power is needed. If the seas turn flat, loosening the battens will flatten out the sail and put you in "high gear." After the battens are set, then the downhaul can be adjusted to see how it affects the evened-up draft. Contrary to popular belief, batten tension really has little to do with shifting pocket position.

DOWNHAUL

By increasing downhaul tension, the pocket of the sail is moved forward and draft depth is increased slightly. Decreasing downhaul tension allows the draft to move aft. When adjusting the downhaul, remember that it's got to be kept tight enough to discourage major luff wrinkles when the sail is sheeted in. Draft position also changes according to the wind strength. As the wind increases, the draft moves aft. The downhaul should be fairly loose in light air, then as the wind increases, it should be tensioned to keep the draft in the same position (between 30 and 40 percent aft of the sail's leading edge). When tuning your sail on land, remember that without wind the pocket might not look good. Try to anticipate the wind and sailing conditions you'll be sailing in. A sail that looks great on land with no wind might look bad on the water in a breeze, and vice versa.

JIB LUFF TENSION

On many sloop-rigged cats, the draft of the jib can be controlled just like the main. Draft in the jib should be kept at 30 to 40 percent aft of its leading edge. If the draft is in the forward 30 percent of the sail in light winds, the luff adjuster needs to be eased so the sail will take on a wider curve. If the draft moves back beyond 40 percent in heavy air, luff tension should be increased to move the draft forward.

OUTHAUL

On footed mains (where the foot of the mainsail is attached to the boom) outhaul tension has little effect on sailshape. To set the outhaul, just pull it out until the wrinkles along the foot of the main disappear. Many cat sailors go around with too much outhaul tension, which puts a crease in the sail along the foot.

The outhaul is very important, however, on loose-footed mainsails where the foot of the sail is attached only at the tack and clew. When beating, the outhaul should be kept tight until power is needed. It also pays to loosen the outhaul when reaching and running, since a real fiat sail is not needed for off the wind sailing. Like all other tuning adjustments the key to finding the correct outhaul tension is to experiment in a variety of conditions.

SAILSHAPE CORRECTION

After playing around with your batten tension, downhaul, and outhaul, you may find that your sail's shape still doesn't look right. Despite valiant efforts, you might still be plagued by draft irregularity, bad pocket position or draft depth. This situation might require a visit to a sailmaker, either for a new sail or a re-cutting of your old one. Sometimes though, it's your battens instead of your sail that need attention. Changing or tapering your battens can really affect the sail.

Having a sail re-cut is an expensive proposition. So be careful when you decide a sail needs alteration. If you're concerned about the position of the pocket, measure it. What may look like a 50-percent pocket position may actually be a perfect 35 percent after all.

Checking and recording sailshape can be done by turning your cat on her side on land with the sails up. Sheet the sails in,

Figure 3

and then lead strings, or a straight edge, from the mast directly to the outer tips of the battens. Taking a stick or a ruler, you can run along the string and determine exactly where the deepest part of the sail is (figure 3). If each batten reveals a 30- to 40-percent draft (pocket) position, the sail is o.k. This measuring technique can also show you if your sail has a gradual and even curve across it from its leading edge to leech.

If you find irregularities in your sail, some kind of attention is necessary. Sometimes you may only have to shave down or replace a batten; other times a major re-cutting may be needed. The latter is unlikely, however, unless your sail has been abused or was built wrong in the first place.

A common draft problem is one sail panel being different from the others. One panel may have a much shallower draft than the others, or it may have a pocket position of 45 percent when the rest of the sail is 35 percent. Both problems might be corrected by planing down the batten nearest the problem area, which will make for a fuller panel. If a certain panel is too full, then a new, stiffer batten will help. Even wrapping a batten with tape will stiffen it and help produce a flatter panel. Experimenting with sail shape and battens should be done carefully. If you're going to stiffen or shave a batten, do it a little bit at a time.

HELM

Once the sails are in good shape, the next tuning step is achieving a proper helm. The first thing to check are your rudders.

They should be perfectly aligned with your hulls. Alignment can be checked by measuring the distance between the leading edges of the rudder blades. The distance should be exactly the same as the distance between the trailing edges of the rudder blades. If the leading edges are closer together than the trailing edges, your rudders are "toed" inwards. This can be corrected with a rudder alignment kit, a longer tiller crossbar, or by expanding your present tiller crossbar if your cat has one that will expand. Sailing around with your rudders toed outwards is also bad—it's like having a parking brake on. If your rudders are toed outwards, the best solution is to either cut or collapse the tiller crossbar until the rudders come back into alignment.

MAST RAKE AND HELM

When your cat tends to head up into the wind, it has weather helm. If you let your tiller go and your cat starts diving off to leeward, it has *leeward helm*. Mast rake is the key to weather or leeward helm. Forward mast rake causes lee helm and aft mast rake causes weather helm. A cat mast can be given aft rake by moving the shrouds down on their chainplates and elongating the forestay. For raking forward, loosen up on the shrouds and take up on the forestay. Most cat skippers like to carry weather helm because it makes boat performance easier to predict and it tends to discourage drag. Lee helm, on the other hand, is a terrible thing to have. It makes upwind sailing difficult, reaches become dangerous, excessive drag is created most of the time, and if you fall overboard, lee helm will encourage your cat to run away.

TILLER LOAD

If your helm is still biased either to windward or to leeward after adjusting your mast rake, or it just feels heavy or sluggish, you might need to counterbalance the rudders. While counterbalancing doesn't actually change your helm, it does change its feeling. This "feeling" is called *tiller load* (if you sail with one rudder up, you'll feel a lot of tiller load). Tiller load can be increased by cocking the rudder tips aft. Load is decreased by cocking the tips forward (figure 4). If you've got too much or too little rudder load, then experimentation with the rudder tips is a must. By moving the transom gudgeons fore and aft

NORMAL NON-
COUNTERBALANCED
RUDDER

COUNTERBALANCED
RUDDER —
LESS TILLER LOAD

Figure 4

with washers, rudder tip angle can be adjusted. Adding washers to the top gudgeons will move the rudder tops backwards and the rudder tips forwards, decreasing the load. To increase rudder load, add washers to the bottom gudgeons. By testing with a variety of settings, you can balance your helm perfectly. Once you find the perfect angle, re-drill the holes in the rudders and put them back on without the washers.

MAST RAKE AND GEARING

Besides raking your mast for correcting helm problems, you can also rake it to reduce underwater drag. By raking aft, drag is reduced because the force of the sailplan is directed to the stern sections of the hulls rather than the fuller bow sections. But raking aft also gives the hulls less thrust and more lift causing a loss of power. So what's best, fore or aft rake? It depends on several things. If you've got a heavier crew or choppy seas to deal with, raking forward helps. Lighter crew weight and smooth seas call for aft mast rake. Aft mast rake also helps if you want to point your highest, since drag reduction doesn't outweigh the benefits of lift. In really heavy air, raking aft reduces the forward pressure of the sails and creates a lifting force in the hulls that helps prevent pitch pole capsizes.

DIAMOND WIRES

Diamond wires are used on racing cats with very tall or thin masts. Adjusted at their lower ends, they affect mast curve and help keep the mast from bending excessively (figure 5). By tightening the diamond wires, you get a straighter mast that produces a fuller mainsail for more power. Reduce the tension and you get more curve, a flatter sail, and less power (figure 6).

INTERMEDIATE TUNING

Figure 5

Figure 6

If you are unable to rake your mast aft as much as you'd like, try a combination of aft rake and loosened diamond wires. Aft mast rake and tightened diamonds will help if you're sailing in choppy seas where the wind has remained moderate. But remember to avoid extremes when you're experimenting; diamond wires that are too loose or too tight can lead to a dismasting. If you're walking by another cat that has diamond wires, check the tension to get an idea of how other cats are tuned. It also helps to ask racing sailors about diamond tuning.

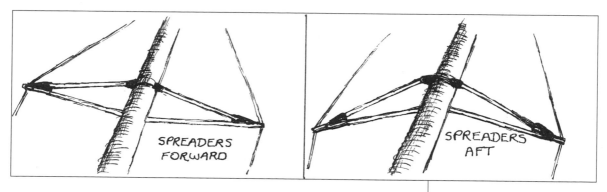

Figure 7

You'll hear a lot of different ideas, but the whole rigging picture should become clearer, too.

SPREADER ANGLE

Diamond wires require spreaders, which can also be experimented with (figure 7). Raking spreaders fore and aft also affect mast bend. Aft spreader rake allows the mast to bend to leeward and increases aft mast bend. Forward spreader rake does the opposite. Like diamond wires, spreaders should always be set evenly on both sides of the mast.

MAST ROTATION

Sail shape can also be changed by mast rotation. A well-rotated mast fairs the mast curve into the leeward side of the mainsail, reducing wind drag. Mast rotation is also another factor in controlling mast bend. The more a mast rotates, the more it bends. Less mast rotation produces a fuller mainsail and more rotation flattens the mainsail.

Without altering your sails, battens or diamond wire tension, you can control sail shape quite a bit with mast rotation. Mast rotation plays its biggest role at the top third of the mast where diamond wire tension is less effective. This portion of most catamaran masts is unstayed, so the slightest amount of sheet tension and wind pressure against the mainsail leech causes aft mast bend. With more mast rotation, you can flatten out the top of the mainsail and free off the leech, which makes for a faster sail in heavy air.

As a rule, 60 to 90 degrees to either side is the minimum and maximum that a mast should be rotated. When you're reaching or going downwind, your mast should be rotated

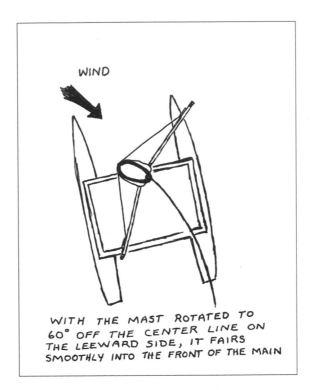

WIND

WITH THE MAST ROTATED TO 60° OFF THE CENTER LINE ON THE LEEWARD SIDE, IT FAIRS SMOOTHLY INTO THE FRONT OF THE MAIN

Figure 8

about 90 degrees. Going upwind, 60 to 80 degrees is the acceptable range (figure 8).

Many sloop-rigged cats will have a point of rotation where the spreaders will catch on the leech of the jib. Whenever this occurs, just increase or decrease the rotation slightly until the jib is free.

If your cat has a rotating mast but it is not adjustable, you might want to file the rotation stops to get the amount of turn you need. Hobie 14 and 16 sailors do this in stages until their masts over-rotate just enough so they get the right amount of mast bend for crew weight and sail shape. In heavy winds, you want enough rotation so you can bend the mast and flatten out the mainsail. Generally, heavier crews want less rotation than lighter crews.

Having a flat main is the way to go both in heavy and light winds. In heavy air you don't need the power of a full main, and in light air the wind has a difficult time passing over and attaching itself to the deep curve of a full main. In moderate air or choppy seas you may not want a flat main, but since you can't control mast rotation beyond filing the mast base stops, there isn't much you can do; this is a compromise you make for a fast sail in other conditions. Increasing batten and downhaul tension can help the problem of a flat main in moderate conditions, but don't expect too much.

As you experiment with rotation (particularly if you have diamond wires) keep an eye on the pocket of your sail and make sure it doesn't drift back past 40 percent. Also watch the leech of your main. A leech that falls off too far to leeward when the sheet is tight will spoil your efforts for a faster cat. Remember that the effects of mast rotation are far more critical on unstayed rigs than on rigs that are stayed and very adjustable.

SHROUD TENSION

Since most cats sail downwind the fastest with the apparent wind at 90 degrees, shroud tension should (usually) be as tight as possible without damaging anything. In cats like the Hobie 16 or Prindle 16s, however, it's the jib luff wire that determines rig tautness. In these cats you don't pay much attention to the shrouds. Instead, keep an eye on the jib pocket position and the overall situation between the main and the jib. The forestay controls the jib pocket position on these cats and is also greatly responsible for harmony between the main and the jib. In lighter winds you should sail with less forestay tension which will loosen the shrouds. In heavy air, tighten the forestay. This will bring the shrouds tight and keep the jib pocket in the correct forward position.

In small una-rigged cats like the Hobie 14, mast rake and shroud tension are an inseparable system. Ideally, the mast should be raked forward off the wind and aft while sailing upwind. If you keep your shrouds loose, you can adjust the rig for these positions by rigging a line from the forestay to the forward crossbar. Pull the line tight when sailing downwind and release it when headed upwind. While carrying tight shrouds restricts mast adjustment, they do help upwind performance by keeping the mast from leaning to leeward, which lets wind spill off the sail. And if you're a heavy skipper, you should have tight shrouds all the time, since you can't afford to spill any wind. Lighter sailors can get away with carrying loose shrouds, since they have to spill wind one way or another while sailing upwind in a heavy breeze. Sailing downwind in light air, heavy sailors with tight shrouds will have a tough time staying up with light sailors, but when it really begins to howl the heavy sailors will dominate.

11/
RACING: RULES AND PREPARATION

For most people, there is nothing more confusing than watching Catamarans race—bunches of multi-colored cats zipping all around, guns firing, then finally they go dancing off in what seems like all different directions. But with just a little

studying, understanding what's going on during a race is pretty easy.

All the boats start together, sail around some buoys, and the boat that goes the fastest and makes the least mistakes crosses the finish line first. The course you sail during a race is an imaginary path on the water, marked off by orange flags or buoys. Sometimes islands or anchored ships are used for racing marks. Whatever is used, the idea is to get the fleet to sail on several points of sail during the race.

The marks must be rounded in a specific order as indicated by a course chart or the race committee. A typical course chart, with the marks identified by letters, might read: "A–B–C–A–C–F, all marks left to port."

The most popular course that is raced is called the Olympic Triangle (figure 1). This triangle has three marks. Mark "A" would be the weather mark, mark "B" the reaching mark, and mark "C" would be the leeward mark. Races almost always start to weather. The course A–B–C–A–C–F would be: beat, reach, reach, beat, run, sail to finish. This way, skippers and crews are tested on all points of sail.

In most races, all the marks must be rounded to port, meaning you must keep them on your left side as you go around them.

The starting line is set by the race committee. It can be set at any corner on the racing triangle, but is usually set near the downwind end, between A and C. The starting line consists of two marks, one is usually the committee boat itself and the other is a movable flag or buoy. A good race committee will shift the flag or buoy around until the wind is blowing 90 degrees to the starting line. Despite a race committee's best efforts, however, the line is usually not "square," which means one end is better to start at than the other.

STARTING A RACE

The rules say a boat has started the instant any part of its hull or gear crosses the starting line. The boats that move out to an early lead always start at the favored end of the line at full speed—something that's harder to do than you might think. The starting gun is fired after a series of timed warnings, usually three: a warning, a preparatory, and the start. White, blue and red flags are also used. A starting sequence usually goes like

RACING: RULES
AND PREPARATION

Figure 1

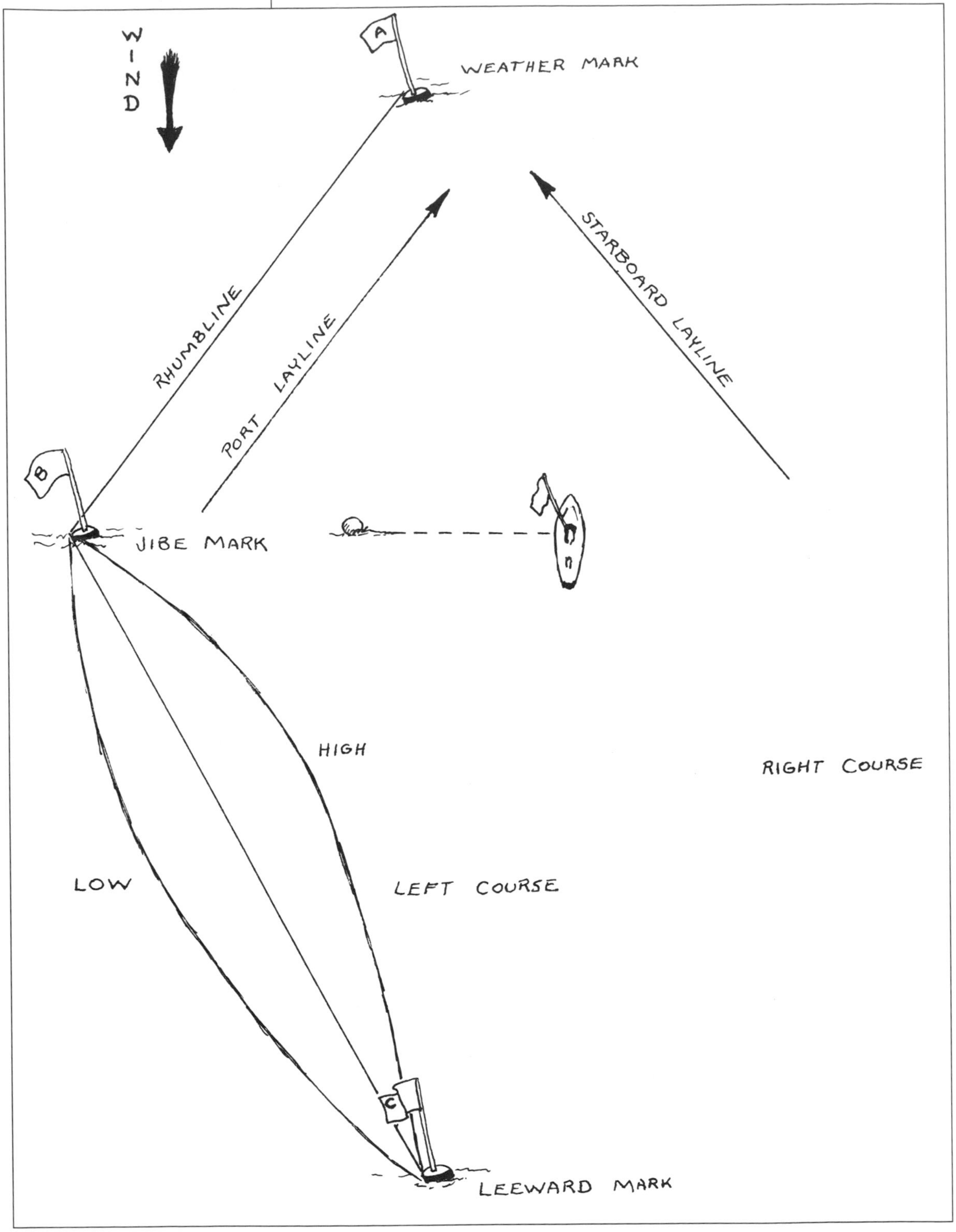

WIND

A

WEATHER MARK

RHUMBLINE

PORT LAYLINE

STARBOARD LAYLINE

B

JIBE MARK

HIGH

RIGHT COURSE

LOW

LEFT COURSE

C

LEEWARD MARK

MASTERING
THE FINE POINTS

this: A horn is blasted repeatedly to get your attention. Thirty seconds later, and ten minutes before the start, the white warning flag goes up. If you have a stop watch, you start it when the flag is hoisted. The white flag stays up for exactly four minutes and thirty seconds, followed by a 30-second period of no flags. Then exactly five minutes after the white flag went up, the preparatory (usually blue) flag goes up. This tells you there is five minutes before the start. Like the warning flag, the preparatory flag stays up four minutes and 30 seconds. When the preparatory flag comes down, there is 30 seconds to go until the starting gun. At the start, a gun or a horn goes off and the red starting flag is hoisted. In some races a gun or horn goes off as each flag goes up, but don't count on it. You've got to watch the flags. If you are over the line when the red flag goes up, the race committee will call out your number and you must re-start the race, keeping clear of other boats while you do it.

RULES

One thing you can be sure of during a race: you'll be sailing very close to other boats. And each time two boats start getting close, one of them has the right of way and the other doesn't. There are rules for every situation, whether you are crossing a boat, taking a boat's stern, or sailing along parallel. You've got to know the rules. And if you foul another boat during the race, the only way you can keep from being thrown out of the race is to sail in two circles. This is called, appropriately enough, "doing a 720." If someone cries foul but you disagree, be prepared for a protest. A protest, held on land after the racing is over, is a kind of court session where both parties present their case to an impartial protest committee. A skipper who wants to protest someone must fill out a protest form immediately after coming ashore.

There are over 80 yacht racing rules established by the United States Yacht Racing Union (USYRU). Another yacht racing organization the International Yacht Racing Union (IYRU) also has dozens of rules. If you're thinking about getting into racing, buy a USYRU or IYRU rule book so you can study up on the rules that govern your specific area. USYRU rules are used in the United States and IYRU rules are used at most regattas in the rest of the world.

Learning all the rules is not necessary for the beginner to

OVERLAPPING CATS

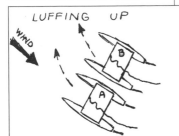

CATS ARE OVERLAPPING WHEN NEITHER CAT IS CLEAR AHEAD.

CLOSE HAULED

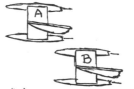

A CAT IS CLOSE HAULED WHEN ITS SAIL IS IN CLOSE AND THE CAT IS POINTING. A CAT CLOSE HAULED IS ALSO CONSIDERED HARD ON THE WIND.

OVERTAKING

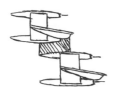

CAT "B" IS OVERTAKING CAT "A"

LUFFING UP

THE ACT OF ALTERING COURSE UNTIL HEAD TO WIND. CAT "A" IS LUFFING CAT "B".

BEARING AWAY

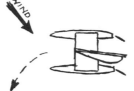

THE PROCESS OF FALLING AWAY FROM THE WIND

PROPER COURSE

PROPER COURSE IS THE COURSE THE CAT WOULD TAKE IF THERE WERE NO OTHER CATS RACING. IN GENERAL, IT'S THE SHORTEST POSSIBLE COURSE TO THE MARK.

TACKING

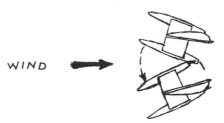

A CAT IS TACKING WHEN IT CROSSES HEAD TO WIND

JIBING

A CAT IS JIBING WHEN ITS BOOM CROSSES ITS CENTERLINE

WINDWARD & LEEWARD

CAT "A" IS LEEWARD
CAT "B" IS WINDWARD

CLEAR AHEAD

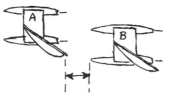

A CAT IS CLEAR AHEAD WHEN NO BOATS OVERLAP IT, AND NO BOATS ARE AHEAD OF IT. CAT "A" IS CLEAR AHEAD OF CAT "B".

ON A CERTAIN TACK

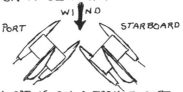

A CAT IS ON A TACK EXCEPT WHEN TACKING OR JIBING. YOU ARE ON A PORT TACK WHEN YOUR SAIL IS ON THE STARBOARD SIDE. WHEN THE SAIL IS ON THE PORT SIDE YOU ARE ON A STARBOARD TACK.

enjoy racing and get around the race course successfully. The beginner does want to know the important rules, the ones that come into play often. If you're out on the race course and some guy starts shouting a rule at you and you're not sure about it, give way. You'll soon pass him anyway since he probably won't be concentrating on what's important—sailing fast in the right direction.

In your first race you should know that a boat on starboard tack has the right of way over a boat on port tack. If one boat is to leeward of another boat, the leeward boat has the right of way. And a cat clear astern has to avoid a cat that is clear

STARBOARD TACK

WIND

STARBOARD TACK HAS RIGHT-OF-WAY OVER A PORT TACK CAT. YOU ARE ON STARBOARD TACK WHEN THE WIND IS BLOWING OVER YOUR STARBOARD (RIGHT) SIDE. THE PORT TACK CAT MUST STAY CLEAR OF THE RIGHT-OF-WAY CAT. (BLACK CAT IN DIAGRAM IS STARBOARD)

LEEWARD CAT

WIND

LEEWARD CAT

LEEWARD CAT HAS RIGHT-OF-WAY OVER A WINDWARD CAT. THE WINDWARD CAT MUST STAY CLEAR WITH ONE EXCEPTION: IF THE WINDWARD CAT, WHILE GOING AROUND A MARK, IS THE INSIDE CAT.

TACKING OR JIBING

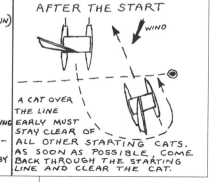

A CAT WHILE TACKING OR JIBING SHALL KEEP CLEAR OF A CAT ON A TACK. IF TWO CATS ARE TACKING OR JIBING AT THE SAME TIME THE CAT ON THE OTHER'S PORT SIDE SHALL KEEP CLEAR.

WIND

OVERTAKING

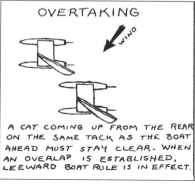

WIND

A CAT COMING UP FROM THE REAR ON THE SAME TACK AS THE BOAT AHEAD MUST STAY CLEAR. WHEN AN OVERLAP IS ESTABLISHED, LEEWARD BOAT RULE IS IN EFFECT.

BARGING
(BEFORE THE STARTING GUN)

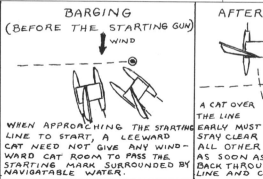

WIND

WHEN APPROACHING THE STARTING LINE TO START, A LEEWARD CAT NEED NOT GIVE ANY WINDWARD CAT ROOM TO PASS THE STARTING MARK SURROUNDED BY NAVIGATABLE WATER.

AFTER THE START

WIND

A CAT OVER THE LINE EARLY MUST STAY CLEAR OF ALL OTHER STARTING CATS. AS SOON AS POSSIBLE, COME BACK THROUGH THE STARTING LINE AND CLEAR THE CAT.

SAME TACK

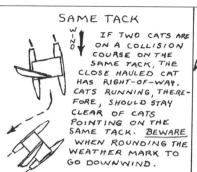

WIND

IF TWO CATS ARE ON A COLLISION COURSE ON THE SAME TACK, THE CLOSE HAULED CAT HAS RIGHT-OF-WAY. CATS RUNNING, THEREFORE, SHOULD STAY CLEAR OF CATS POINTING ON THE SAME TACK. BEWARE WHEN ROUNDING THE WEATHER MARK TO GO DOWNWIND.

SEA ROOM (SAME TACK)

IF TWO OR MORE CATS ARE ON THE SAME TACK GOING AROUND A MARK THE CAT TO THE INSIDE, OVERLAPPING CATS AHEAD OR TO THE OUTSIDE, HAS THE RIGHT-OF-WAY GOING AROUND THE MARK, AND THE OUTSIDE CAT MUST GIVE ROOM.

HAS RIGHT OF WAY

SEA ROOM (OPPOSITE TACK)

WIND

THE CAT ON STARBOARD TACK HAS RIGHT-OF-WAY OVER A PORT TACK CAT.

ON THE DOWNWIND LEG THE INSIDE OVERLAPPING CAT, REGARDLESS OF TACK, HAS RIGHT-OF-WAY AROUND THE MARK.

RACING: RULES
AND PREPARATION

ahead. These are the basic rules you should be aware of at the beginning of your racing career. The more you race, the more rules you'll learn.

PRE-RACE PREPARATION

When you arrive at a regatta, you'll need every minute to rig up, check the weather, go to the skipper's meeting, and most importantly, get out on the water and check the current and wind. This means that your cat should be perfectly tuned and ready to race before the regatta.

On the morning of the race, you should check the weather report and note the expected wind velocity and direction. If you notice the wind direction begin to move toward the direction the weather report has indicated, you've already got a good idea what's going to happen on the race course weatherwise.

Also ask the locals about the weather. Lifeguards, fishermen, surfers and other waterfront locals usually have a good idea what the weather will do in their area.

THE SKIPPER'S MEETING

At the skipper's meeting you find out crucial things. Like the starting sequence, types of marks to be used, and specifics about the courses. If you have any questions about the regatta, the skipper's meeting is the time and place to ask. Missing the skipper's meeting can easily cost you the regatta, if as frequently happens, the race committee changes plans or shifts a mark, etc.

GETTING OUT ON THE WATER

While most cat racers don't go out on the water until just before the start, you should get out as soon as you can if you want to do well. By checking the wind, current, and waves, you can develop a strategy for the first beat while your competitors mess around on shore. Sailing out early also allows you some time for any last-minute tuning adjustments that may be necessary. And by standing on deck and hanging on to a shroud, you can take some time to look for the course marks and record their position in your mind. Doing all of these things will make you more prepared. And when you're prepared, you're confident—which is all-important for winning races.

Just before the race begins, try to think about what you're doing and why. Whether you plan to stay with the fleet or sail away from it, you should have good reasons behind your moves. Wind shifts and current should be at the top of your list when deciding which way to go.

WIND MOVEMENT

The wind moves in two ways—it is either *veering* or *hauling*. Veering is when the wind is moving clockwise and hauling is when it is moving counter clockwise (figure 2). When the wind veers or hauls, it does so until it settles to a constant direction. Sometimes a wind will be veering for hours, other times it will veer for a few minutes.

When relating wind shifts to your cat, the terms *header* and *lift* are used. A header is a wind shift that moves towards your bow, causing you to either sheet in or fall off. When racing upwind, a leeward cat gains over a windward cat in a header (figure 3). A lift is a windshift that moves away from your bow, causing you to sheet out or head up. When racing upwind, a windward cat gains over a leeward cat in a lift (figure 4).

HAULING AND VEERING

Figure 2

Figure 3

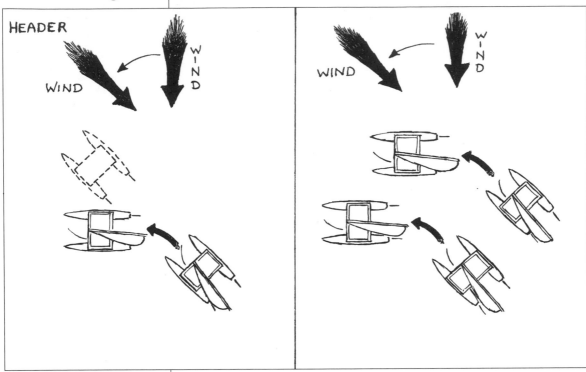

HEADER

WIND   WIND

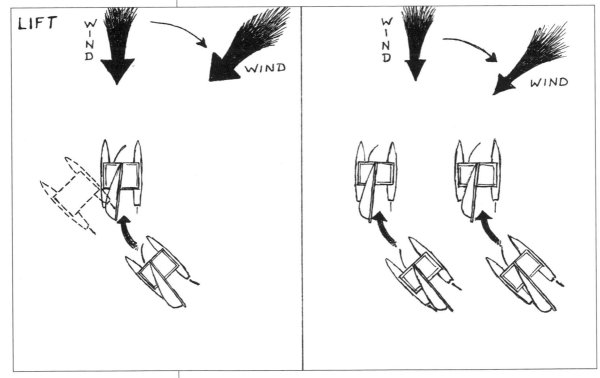

LIFT   WIND   WIND   WIND   WIND

Figure 4

/ 150 /

MASTERING
THE FINE POINTS

When you're sailing you are constantly reacting to headers and lifts since they occur, to some degree, all the time. When they do, one tack will be lifted and the other headed or vice versa. Never, in the same wind, will both port and starboard tacks be lifted or headed.

USING WIND SHIFTS

To sail a good race, you've got to have an idea of how the wind will be shifting on the course. You should know whether the wind is veering or hauling, and you should try to predict what kinds of headers and lifts will be occurring. Basically, you can identify four wind patterns: consistent winds, unpredictable winds, oscillating winds, and persistent winds.

You can figure out which of these patterns is working by sailing closehauled before the start and observing how much you have to change your course in order to stay closehauled. A compass is a valuable tool for this exercise. If you don't have a compass, then try using objects on shore to get relative bearings for detecting wind shifts.

If your heading remains constant on a long tack, you've got a consistent wind. But if you have to change course drastically to keep your cat closehauled, you know that you'll be sailing in unpredictable winds. If your heading slowly rises or drops while closehauled, it's a persistent wind, and a persistent wind moves in just one direction during a leg. Finally, if you find that your heading changes from a lift to a header in a predictable cyclic pattern while on a long tack, you've discovered an oscillating wind. This kind of wind pattern shifts back and forth during a leg, and the duration of the shifts is regular.

WORKING THE CONSISTENT AND UNPREDICTABLE WINDS

If you have detected a consistent or unpredictable wind before the start, you should plan to sail first on the tack that heads you closer to the windward mark. A racing rule: when you are in doubt about which tack to sail on always sail on the tack that takes you closest to the mark. Once you have decided which tack is the one you want, you should be on it as soon as possible after the gun goes off.

Sailing on the tack that takes you closest to the mark gives

RACING: RULES
AND PREPARATION

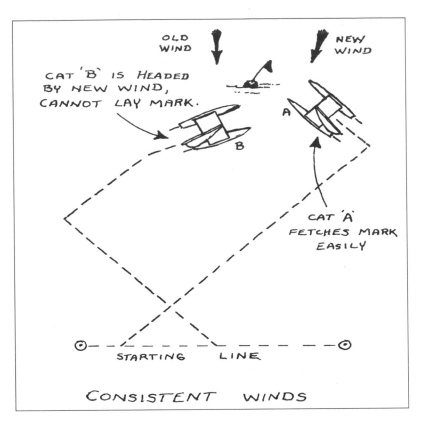

OLD WIND

NEW WIND

CAT 'B' IS HEADED BY NEW WIND, CANNOT LAY MARK.

A

B

CAT 'A' FETCHES MARK EASILY

STARTING LINE

CONSISTENT WINDS

Figure 5

you a couple of advantages in consistent or unpredictable winds. First, if the wind shifts in your favor (lifts you) you can sail even closer towards the weather mark (figure 5). And if the wind shifts against you (a header) just tack and you'll be on the lifted tack since a header on one tack means a lift on the other.

WORKING THE PERSISTENT WIND

If you've decided that you'll be starting in a persistent wind, it usually pays to sail on the headed tack first—the tack that takes you further away from the windward mark. As you do this, your heading will get progressively worse. Which of course means the other tack will be getting better. Stay on the headed tack until you can tack on the layline (where you can sail straight for the mark). Whatever you do, don't tack too early for the mark or sail on the lifted tack after the start. Either situation would cause you to tack into an increasing header during the progressively shifting wind, which means you would be sailing unnecessary distance (figure 6).

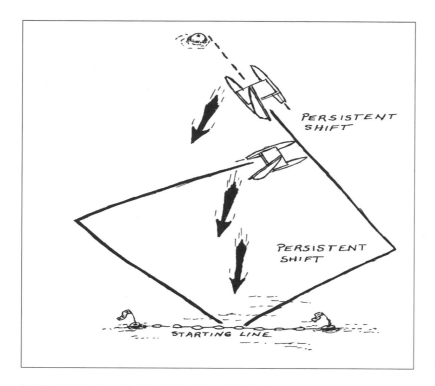

Figure 6

WORKING THE OSCILLATING WIND

With an oscillating wind at the start you should sail on the lifted tack first—the tack that takes you closest to the windward mark. You never want to sail off to one side of the course in an oscillating wind. Also avoid sailing on a headed tack for too long since your competition on the opposite tack is being lifted while you're headed. If you sail too far to one side of the course, you may end up coming back into the fleet on a header—which is nothing short of disastrous. You may also end up overstanding the weather mark if the wind lifts you after you've sailed too far off to a "corner" of the course. Over-standing (going further than you need to before tacking for the mark) can cost you a lot of distance and boats. In an oscillating wind you want to tack on the headers and keep on the lifts as long as possible (figure 7).

CURRENT

Compared to wind shifts, current is simple to understand and deal with. Since current decreases in shallower water and runs the strongest where it is deepest, you want to sail in shallow water while going against the current and in deep water when

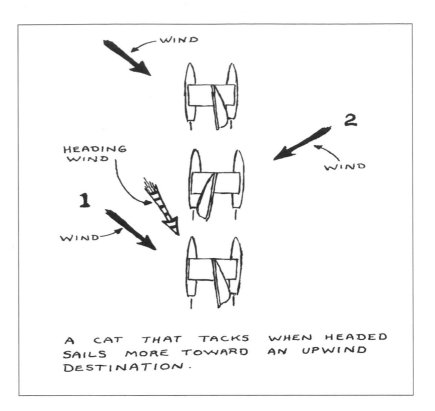

A CAT THAT TACKS WHEN HEADED SAILS MORE TOWARD AN UPWIND DESTINATION.

Figure 7

you're headed with it. Normally though, wind shifts should be your primary consideration when deciding where to go. But the stronger the current, the more you must consider it when developing your race plans.

Use the weather report and a tide table for determining the current in the race area. When you're racing in a bay, the current will run with the tide. When you're on the water, look at buoys and moored boats as you go by them. Often a moored boat will be headed into the current if the wind is not a significant factor. The best way to see current though is to look at the water go around a buoy or mark. If there is a strong current (or tide) you'll see a wake leaving the buoy. And if you see water churning around a buoy, you should really give the current a lot of thought.

FORM A PLAN

After checking out the wind and current, you should be forming a plan about how you are going to reach the weather mark after the start. Start by asking yourself, "What would be the quickest way to go without the interference of my competitors?" If you can answer this question, making your weather leg plan will be a lot easier. Figuring out the right way to go will also help you decide where to start on the line, since you should start in what you feel is the best direction to achieve your plan.

THE START PLAN

At the warning signal (white flag) the race committee will post the course. With the aid of your course chart, you should memorize the marks and the sequence you'll have to round them. Then check the starting line and decide which end of it is furthest up wind, i.e., the favored end.

One way to determine the favored end is to luff your cat in to the wind right in the middle of the line and sight the angle between your heading and the line (figure 8). Another method is to sail down the line carrying a slight luff in your mainsail. Keeping the sheet at the same setting jibe around and head back along the line in the opposite direction. The favored end is the one where your mainsail luffs the most when you head for it. If the luffing is equal on both tacks, then you've got an even line and you can start anywhere without giving up distance to your competitors.

Figure 8

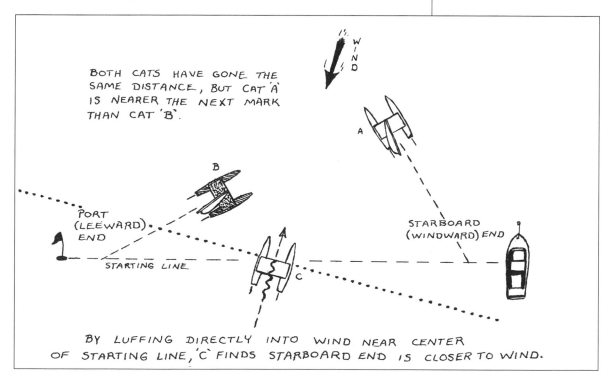

BOTH CATS HAVE GONE THE SAME DISTANCE, BUT CAT 'A' IS NEARER THE NEXT MARK THAN CAT 'B'.

WIND

B

A

PORT (LEEWARD) END

STARBOARD (WINDWARD) END

STARTING LINE

C

BY LUFFING DIRECTLY INTO WIND NEAR CENTER OF STARTING LINE, 'C' FINDS STARBOARD END IS CLOSER TO WIND.

RACING: RULES
AND PREPARATION

One thing you will notice is that you won't be alone at the favored end of the line. Most of your competitors can figure out which end is best too. And the more one end of the line is favored, the more congested that end will be.

If the starting line favors a port tack start, think twice before attempting it. In a fleet of any size, you'll most likely get caught by a starboard tack boat. Unless the line so favors a port tack start that the whole fleet is on port, you'd better play it safe and start on starboard tack near the port end (figure 9).

Your starting plan should complement your weather leg plan if possible. Think about where you want to be about two minutes after the start. If you want to be going off on port tack towards an eventual header, it's not wise to start way down on the port end of the line even if it's favored. This is because you'll have the whole fleet behind you on starboard tack and you'll be trapped until your competitors tack first. You would be better off to start two-thirds or halfway down the line, where the chances of being able to tack quickly after the start are better.

If your plan calls for getting away from the fleet and finding clear air, then starting at the extreme end of the line is often the way to go. Regardless of your plan, you've got to have clear air and room to sail fast during and after the start. Sometimes getting these things means sacrificing that perfect start.

Figure 9

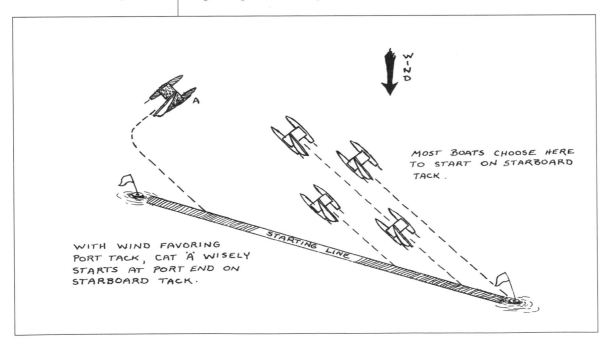

WIND

MOST BOATS CHOOSE HERE TO START ON STARBOARD TACK.

STARTING LINE

WITH WIND FAVORING PORT TACK, CAT 'A' WISELY STARTS AT PORT END ON STARBOARD TACK.

MASTERING
THE FINE POINTS

13/
RACING TACTICS

While getting your cat to go fast is a primary consideration during a race, there are going to be some problems when you try to achieve this goal—your competitors. You might be able to figure out the fastest course to the weather mark, but chances are the guys around you won't make it easy to sail that course. Tactics are your defense here. And if you want to go on the offense against a competitor you have to beat to win, your tactics, or the lack of them, will often decide the outcome.

BACKWIND AND BLANKET

The primary reason you want a good start is avoiding the backwind, or dirty air, left by other cats. While you're sailing on that first beat to the weather mark, you'll have cats tacking all around you and many of them will be tacking "on" your clean wind, slowing you down. To keep these intrusions down to a minimum you've got to understand the dynamics of backwind and blanketing.

The windward flow of air across your sails creates disturbed air that trails behind and extends up to weather behind your cat. If you have a competitor directly behind you, or behind and to weather of you, he is sailing in your bad air. Sailing in someone's bad air slows you down and so does sailing

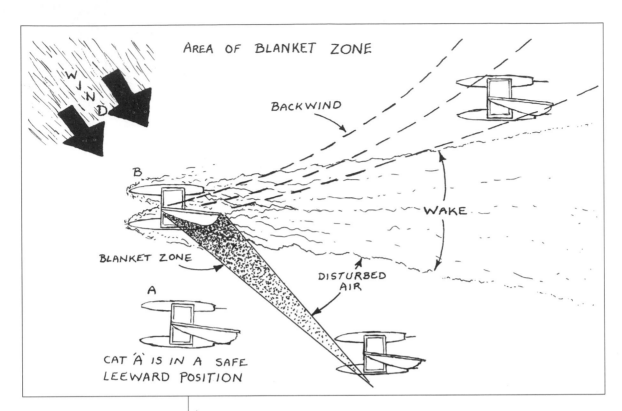

AREA OF BLANKET ZONE

WIND

BACKWIND

WAKE

B

BLANKET ZONE

DISTURBED AIR

A

CAT 'A' IS IN A SAFE
LEEWARD POSITION

Figure 1

in someone's wake. You have two choices to get out of the situation: tack away, or fall off and sail below the offending boat. If you fall off successfully, you will get a *safe leeward* position, where you are abeam of your competitor and no longer getting his backwind (figure 1).

A blanket zone exists to leeward of every sailboat. This zone contains wind that is severely bent and slowed in velocity. The extent of the blanket zone depends on the size of the boat's rig and the wind velocity. When you're in someone's blanket zone, you have to fall off and gain speed or tack away. Otherwise you'll fall further behind.

Intentional blanketing happens all the time during a race, especially downwind. Trying to blanket someone as you sail downwind can be tricky however, since the exact position of the zone is hard to discern. You may be sailing directly upwind of your competitor and not be blanketing him at all (figure 2).

If you want to blanket a competitor while you are broad reaching, you must move well to windward before you can bother his wind. This also means that when you're reaching, you don't have to worry about being blanketed by a cat that's directly astern.

MASTERING
THE FINE POINTS

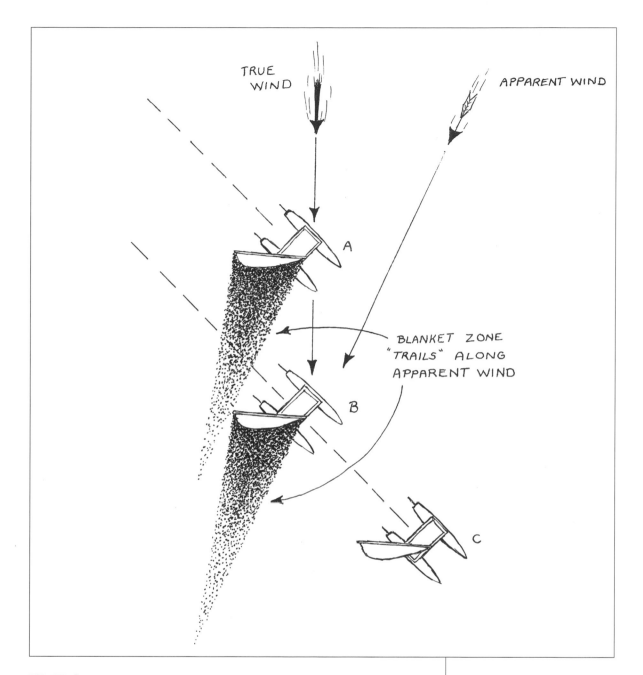

TRUE WIND

APPARENT WIND

A

B

C

BLANKET ZONE "TRAILS" ALONG APPARENT WIND

THE START

As the seconds walk across your watch and you approach the starting line, your main concern should be getting a clear air start on, or very near, the line. You should figure out where you want to be when the gun goes off—and do your best to be there. Try and keep your leeward side clear of other boats as you start. If you do start with a boat to leeward of you, chances

Figure 2

In tightly packed starts like this you've got to fight for clear air!

are you won't be able to fall off and gain speed when the gun goes off since the rules favor the leeward boat, it can do just about anything to keep a windward boat from passing either to windward or to leeward. If you touch a leeward boat, you've fouled.

Naturally, timing is crucial at the start. To arrive at the starting line at exactly the right time takes a lot of practice. Good starters can accurately judge the wind velocity, boat speed, anticipated speed, the approximate length of the line, and, perhaps most importantly, competitor reactions as the start approaches.

If your timing is off and you arrive at the line too soon, you'll be forced to luff (sails flapping) down the line with less-ened maneuverability. This puts you in a defensive position as your competition comes roaring to the line to leeward with more speed. If you arrive late, you will be on the offensive, trying to grab a decent spot in a fleet that is already lined up and thinking defensively to protect its positions.

Wherever you are on the line, the intensity of the start will

MASTERING
THE FINE POINTS

reach a high pitch 30 seconds before the starting gun. Anxious skippers will be fighting for clear air and the less confident sailors will be sitting in irons waiting and wondering what all the yelling is about. Your main concern should be getting your cat moving at full speed when the gun goes off.

In the final 5 to 10 seconds you should check your position in relation to the line. Are you up on the line or sagging way

Cat 266 just got a terrible start. He's boxed in by the cat to weather of him and sailing in the backwind of cat 37. He has no room to maneuver and "dirty air" to boot!

beneath it? If you are on the line, you might have to sheet out and wait for the gun before sheeting in again. If you are below the line with 10 seconds to go, you'd better get moving. Remember, don't get caught without speed when the gun goes off. If you do, your competitors will sail right over you and smother you with dirty air. There's nothing worse than getting blanketed by 15 or 20 cats.

AFTER THE START

The gun has gone off and good or bad? you've started. Are you feeling elated over a perfect start? Or are you ready to chew your mainsheet in half because you let 10 cats sail over the top of you? Are you being taken in the wrong direction by a bunch of skippers who don't know any better? The answers to these questions should determine your tactics during the first windward leg.

WORKING THE LEFT

If you got a clean air start and wanted to be on starboard tack right away, you're in good shape. You probably won't want to tack until you can sail for the windward mark on port tack.

Figure 3

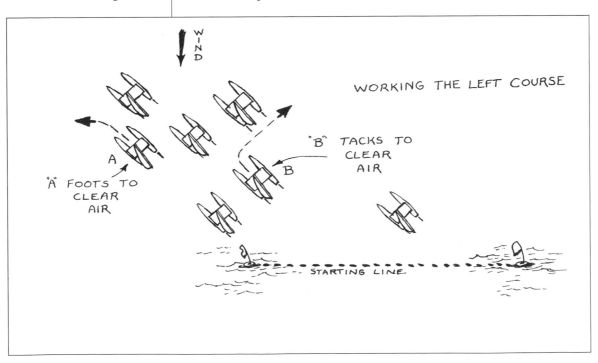

MASTERING
THE FINE POINTS

If you got a poor start but want to stay on starboard tack, you've got to try and clear your air. Even though you may be going in the right direction, the cats above you that are giving you dirty air are really slowing you down. You can do one of two things: tack when it's possible, or fall off and try to gain a safe leeward position (figure 3).

Assuming you want to stay on starboard tack (keeping to the left side of the course), a decision to tack should be based on the duration of the weather leg and the seriousness of your blanketed position. Think twice about tacking. If you tack once, you'll have to tack again to get back on starboard after you've cleared your air. On a long windward leg you might be able to get away with it. But on a short leg, two tacks may cost you more than the exposure to dirty air if you hang in there on starboard tack.

WORKING THE RIGHT

If you planned to get on port tack right after the start and work the right side of the course, try to tack in a spot where other boats will not threaten your air when you're on the new tack. If a couple of boats have tacked just ahead of you, it wouldn't be smart to tack under them. There are situations where every-

Figure 4

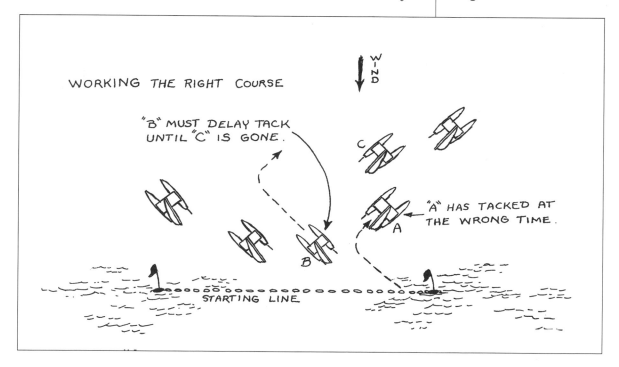

WORKING THE RIGHT COURSE

"B" MUST DELAY TACK UNTIL "C" IS GONE.

"A" HAS TACKED AT THE WRONG TIME.

STARTING LINE

one will tack to port right after the start. A good start can turn in to a disaster if you tack too soon under the boats ahead or too late, letting boats behind you get to the favored side of the course sooner. A poor start can often be overcome by a well-timed tack that gets you going to the right side of the course in clear air (figure 4).

MIDCOURSE TACTICS: WORKING THE RIGHT

If you spend the majority of the weather leg on port tack your most important decision will be when to tack for the mark. In most cases, it's best to hold off until you're sure you can make the mark on starboard tack. You should also, however, consider the fleet. If you're fortunate enough to be ahead, then you can tack when the time is right. But if you're behind, you might have to sail further than necessary to make sure you can "lay" the mark. In every regatta there are boats that tack at the right spot to make the weather mark, but when they get covered by other boats ahead, they end up not being able to make the mark—resulting in two very costly "extra" tacks. It almost always pays to "overstand" the mark a little if you think you could get bad air going towards the weather mark (figure 5).

Figure 5

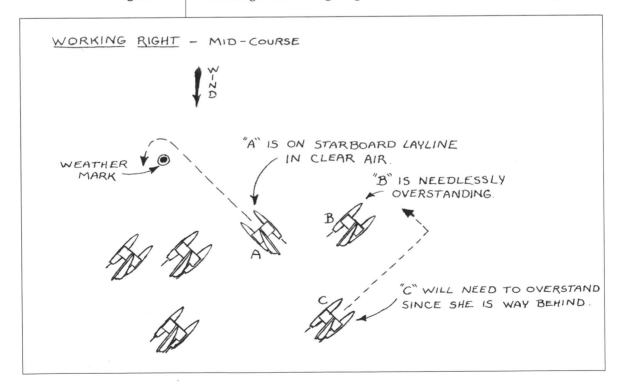

WORKING RIGHT — MID-COURSE

WIND

"A" IS ON STARBOARD LAYLINE IN CLEAR AIR.

"B" IS NEEDLESSLY OVERSTANDING.

WEATHER MARK

A

B

"C" WILL NEED TO OVERSTAND SINCE SHE IS WAY BEHIND.

C

MIDCOURSE TACTICS: WORKING THE LEFT

If you have spent the majority of the windward leg on starboard tack, your most important tactical decision will again be when to tack for the mark. Unless you're in the lead, an early tack is usually the best tactic. By tacking early, you can pick a good spot to tack (to avoid being covered on the new tack) and, after tacking back, you can make your approach to the mark with plenty of speed and the full rights of the starboard tack boat (figure 6). Tacking early can have its drawbacks, however, if the fleet is also tacking early. If you are in the middle of the fleet and tack early, your chances of getting dirty air on the tack to the mark are very good. In such situations, hang on until you can get the cleanest air possible.

APPROACHING THE WEATHER MARK

As you approach the weather mark, you should begin to develop a rough plan for the next leg. Figure out which tack you'll want to be on once you're around, which side of the course looks the best, and how high or low you want to sail if the next leg is a reach.

Figure 6

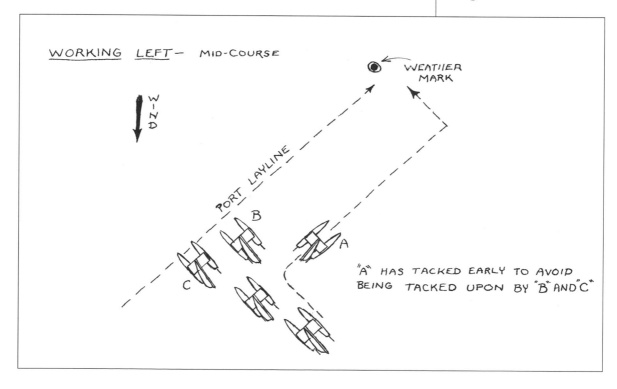

WORKING LEFT— MID-COURSE

WIND

WEATHER MARK

PORT LAYLINE

B

A

C

"A" HAS TACKED EARLY TO AVOID BEING TACKED UPON BY "B" AND "C"

REACHING

The reaching leg is the fastest leg of the course. To generate the most speed on a reach, you've got to stay out of dirty air, which is sometimes a hard thing to do since the fastest course is usually a straight line—meaning there is no way you can tack to avoid dirty air. Everybody tries to pass the boats ahead of them on a reach, which forces all the boats higher and higher as each one tries to keep clean air. By sailing high early in the leg, the fleet ends up dropping off towards the next mark on a much slower heading. When the fleet is forced up in this fashion, reaching tactics require a balance between keeping clear air and sailing the shortest possible distance.

If you are ahead on the beat and round the weather mark without the threat of cats close behind, it's often best to sail low on the course as you begin the reaching leg. Then, if a few boats start to close in on you, you can reach up towards the mark to keep your air clear. But if you're behind or in the middle of the fleet, your only choice is to follow the leaders as they go higher and try and cover the boats behind you (figure 7).

If you're way behind and see the fleet sailing high, then you might consider sailing straight for the next mark since the boats that would cover you are so far ahead that they won't give you

Figure 7

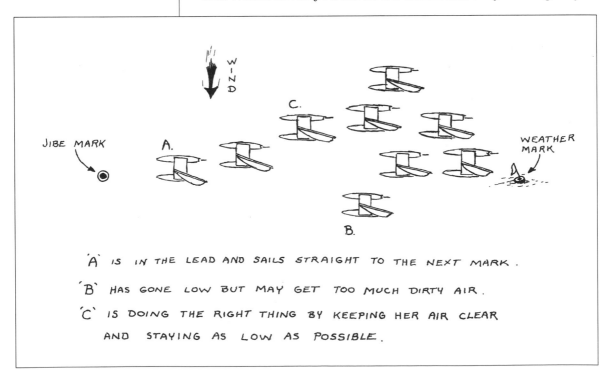

'A' IS IN THE LEAD AND SAILS STRAIGHT TO THE NEXT MARK.

'B' HAS GONE LOW BUT MAY GET TOO MUCH DIRTY AIR.

'C' IS DOING THE RIGHT THING BY KEEPING HER AIR CLEAR
   AND STAYING AS LOW AS POSSIBLE.

MASTERING
THE FINE POINTS

dirty air. This is the one advantage of being behind; you can see mistakes that the leaders are making and avoid them.

RUNNING

Deciding which jibe to be on is the most important decision you make when you begin your downwind leg. Ideally you know which way you want to go a few minutes before reaching the mark. In consistent or unpredictable winds the best tack for the run is the one that carries you closest to the next (leeward) mark. Experienced sailors use a compass to help them make this decision. If you don't have a compass, you can figure out which tack is best by standing up on your cat (after you've rounded the windward mark) and sighting the leeward mark. Which way to go should be pretty obvious. If you're on the wrong tack after rounding the mark, you should jibe immediately. Also keep in mind that you must keep the apparent wind at 90 degrees.

As you approach the windward it's time to develop a strategy for the coming reach or run.

Figure 8

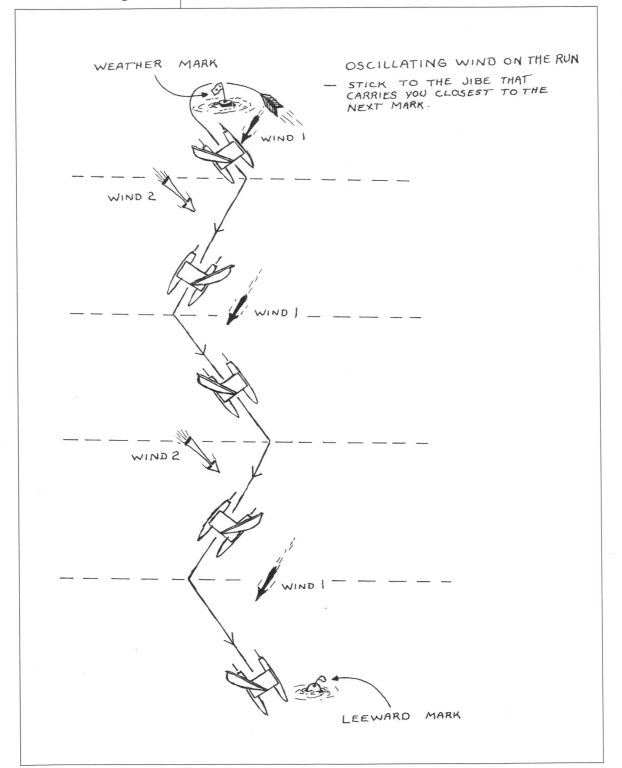

WEATHER MARK

OSCILLATING WIND ON THE RUN
— STICK TO THE JIBE THAT CARRIES YOU CLOSEST TO THE NEXT MARK.

WIND 1

WIND 2

WIND 1

WIND 2

WIND 1

LEEWARD MARK

If the wind was oscillating on the beat, it will probably oscillate on the run. Again, stick to the tack that carries you closest to the leeward mark. In shifty conditions, you can stay on the best tack by jibing on the lifts and staying with the headers (figure 8). This is the opposite way you work such wind shifts sailing upwind, but it does the same thing; keeping you sailing the shortest distance to the next mark.

A persistently moving wind on the beat usually means the wind will continue swinging on the run. In this case, you should sail downwind on the lifted tack first, even if it is taking you away from the leeward mark. When you finally jibe for the

Figure 9

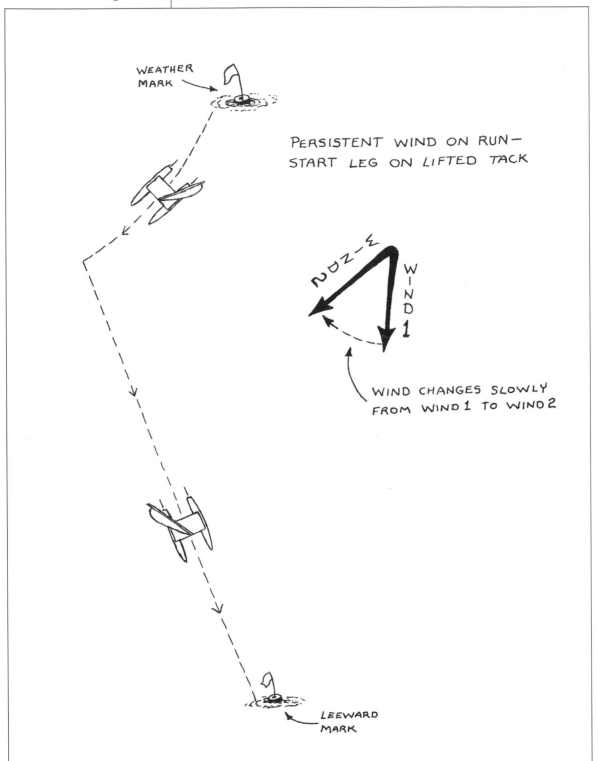

WEATHER MARK

PERSISTENT WIND ON RUN—
START LEG ON LIFTED TACK

WIND 2

WIND 1

WIND CHANGES SLOWLY
FROM WIND 1 TO WIND 2

LEEWARD MARK

mark, you will then be headed, which will make for a fast distance saving course to the mark (figure 9).

ROUNDING THE LEEWARD MARK

Rounding the leeward mark is the most important of all mark roundings in a catamaran race. It is not uncommon to pass other cats during a good mark rounding. And more importantly, a good mark rounding should give you clean air on the second beat. A bad mark rounding can leave you completely covered by other boats and unable to tack in the direction you want to go.

You must plan in advance your leeward mark rounding if you want to do a good job of it. Going into a leeward mark without a game plan will almost always result in your competitors getting the best of you. The first rule is to round inside of other boats if you feel the left side of the course is favored. An inside position allows you to pinch up and tack to the left after rounding the mark. If you're not on the inside, you'll have to wait until the boats above you decide to tack.

Mark rounding tactics should be primarily determined by fleet position if a right course is favored. If, for example, you're

Figure 10

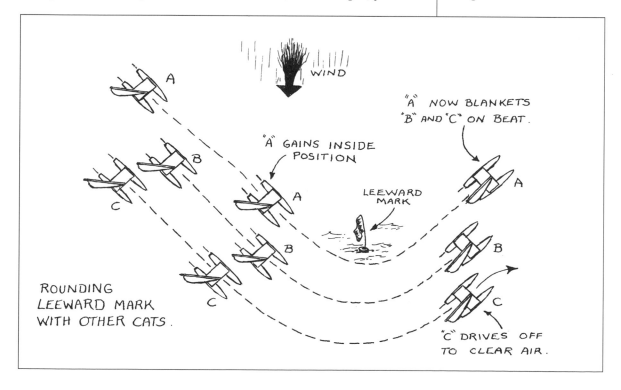

WIND

"A" NOW BLANKETS "B" AND "C" ON BEAT.

"A" GAINS INSIDE POSITION

LEEWARD MARK

ROUNDING LEEWARD MARK WITH OTHER CATS.

"C" DRIVES OFF TO CLEAR AIR.

in fourth place with a large gap between you and the third place cat, you don't have to worry about being backwinded as you round. If you're right behind another cat, you'll want to round the mark just outside your competitor and try and drive through his lee (figure 10). This tactic won't work if there is a bunch of boats ahead of you though, since the projected bad air would be too much to drive through. In this situation, the best thing is to round the mark as close as possible and tack when you can after rounding.

FINISH

When you are rounding a leeward mark and starting the last beat for the finish, you should use the same tactics as you would in any other weather leg. And keep your wits about you as you go for the finish. Many skippers will go after one boat and try and beat it to the finish while three others who were behind will go the right direction and cross the finish line ahead.

Like the starting line, the finish line will almost always have a favored end (figure 11). A good time to check the line out is while you're sailing on the downwind leg. Your last tack(s) to the finish should be influenced by the favored end of the line.

Figure 11

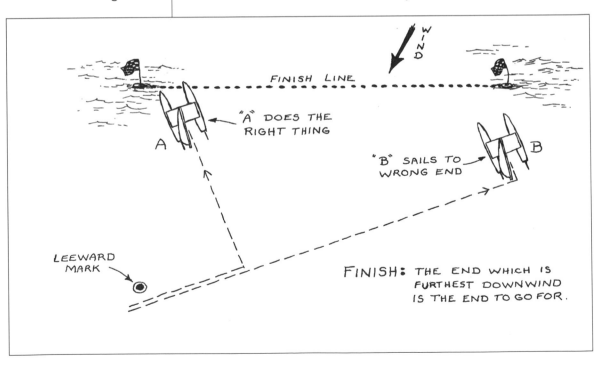

Often there will be boats around you making it difficult to sail the last tack exactly as you would like, however. If this is the case, the only thing to do is try and sail the shortest distance. Some times a couple of cats around you will make the favored end of the line not worth the effort.

CONCLUSION

Racing remains fun as long as you remember that a winner is only a winner if he feels that way. If you are convinced you did your best in a race, it should not really matter that you finished tenth instead of first. And no one jumps on a cat and starts winning right away. Those at the top did a lot of losing before they began to collect their silver. While this chapter may be pretty complex at times, it should help you understand how much is involved in the sport of catamaran racing. There's a lot to it, and the sooner you start thinking about the terms and tactics of racing the sooner your skills will pick up on the race course.

The main thing to remember about racing—and a lot of skippers forget this—is that it's supposed to be fun.

14/
SURFING

More than any other kind of boat, catamarans have popularized the "off the beach" approach to recreational sailing. Some cats are even capable of sailing in and out of large surf, providing the wind is strong and blowing from the right direction.

Your cat's ability to surf is determined by the amount of rocker (lift of the bows and sterns) in its hulls, its ability to sail without centerboards, and the strength of its construction.

Hobie and Prindle cats look somewhat like bananas in profile, sail well without centerboards, and are well built. For these reasons they make the best surf cats.

Consider your cat for surfing. If the hulls have little rocker and it's a light built cat like a Tornado, you really shouldn't ride surf over three feet high. But all cats can surf, either on ocean swells or shoreside breakers. The main thing to know is how much surf you and your cat can handle.

ANATOMY OF A WAVE

Most waves have a peak and a shoulder. The peak is the highest point of a wave. A wave's shoulders are on the left and right sides of the peak. Normally, the shoulders get smaller the farther from the peak they are (figure 1).

Out at sea waves don't break unless they are very large. This is because a wave normally breaks when it reaches half its height in depth to the bottom. So in theory, a six-foot wave will break in three feet of water.

Waves are slowed as they approach the shores that slope

Figure 1

SHOULDER   "PEAK"   SHOULDER

Figure 2

Figure 3

Figure 4

out to sea very gradually. The beaches off Texas are a good example of this. There the waves are slowed to the point where they crumble and become weak in relation to their size. Such waves have small concavity to their faces, well-defined peaks, and slow moving shoulders. Called "mushy," these waves are good for catamaran surfing because "bowdigging" is reduced (figure 2).

A different type of wave exists in Hawaii. The bottom drops off very quickly from the shore off the islands, allowing the waves to move in very fast. These waves break with tremendous power the instant they hit a reef or shelf. Such fast breakers are called tubes (figure 3). The face of a tube is very concave and its lip (top of the curl) is very powerful. Surfers like these kinds of waves because they can ride inside the tube and follow the wave's shoulder as it moves rapidly down the beach. Catamarans can't ride tubes because they can't sail sideways at the steep angle that the wave face forms.

Another type of wave is the "closeout." A closeout can be either tubular or mushy. It has an irregular shoulder and tends to break all at once. Eventually, all waves become closeouts as they roll up to the shore (figure 4).

MASTERING
THE FINE POINTS

SURFING THE SWELL OR MUSHY WAVE

Riding the ocean swell or mushy wave in your cat is pretty simple. Your only concern is pearling (digging the bows under). Pearling often leads to a capsize, but isn't much of a danger unless the wind and swells are high. To avoid a pearl, angle down the wave's face toward the shoulder, move your weight aft or sheet out if the wind is strong. The secret to cat surfing is to stay on the swell by angling down the shoulder and turning back into it as the shoulder becomes flat. By practicing with your weight movement, steering, and sail sheeting, you can get some incredible thrills from surfing your cat.

When sailing into a surfline with breaking waves, follow the same technique for riding swells or mushy waves until the wave turns into a tube or a closeout. You cannot keep up with a tube, and you can't successfully surf a closeout. Trying to stay with these kinds of waves will get you turned over fast. So instead of angling down the side surf these waves by heading in the direction of the breaker. Never turn sideways on a tube or a closeout. As you go straight down the wave, be sure to have all of your weight far aft.

As soon as you arrive at the wave's bottom and begin rid-

ing in the foam, lift up your centerboards if you have them, and make sure your rudders will kick up. When you hit the beach, don't waste any time jumping off and pulling your cat clear of the surf. Once you're safely away from the shoreline, swing your cat into the wind and leave the sails uncleated.

HINTS FOR BEACH SURFING

1. While you should be sailing your cat at full speed when you approach a wave for surfing, never go charging over a steep wave that's about to break since such a maneuver will almost certainly cause you to pearl.
2. When a wave steepens, turn your cat in the direction that the wave is breaking (usually straight towards shore) and shift your weight way aft.
3. When a wave breaks behind you, keep calm and hang on!
4. If you've got centerboards or rudders that don't kick up automatically, be sure to raise them before you hit the beach. If your boards hit the beach at a high rate of speed, serious damage will result.
5. Once on the beach, turn your cat into the wind and uncleat the sail(s).

SAILING OUT THROUGH SURF

Sailing out through surf takes a little more skill than sailing in. The cardinal rule is never to sail out through large surf unless the wind is blowing down the beach or offshore. The wind has to be strong enough to propel you and your cat against and over the waves.

Experienced sailors can usually sail out through the surf in onshore winds, but they know just the right angle to sail at in order to get the needed speed to power out through it. Tacking through the surf is asking for trouble, so until you have it mastered in other conditions, save sailing out through the surf in onshore winds until you're comfortable handling your cat in waves.

If you have offshore or down-the-beach winds and want to sail out, first set your cat up right. Put the tiller extension on the proper side and have your traveler(s) and/or jib barber haulers pre-set (see chapter 7). Once your cat is ready, sit back and watch the surf. You want to sail out during a lull. Waves usually come in sets with a lull period between them. When you spot a lull, quickly push your cat out into the shoreline surge, being careful to keep your bows pointed straight into the on-coming foam. If your cat starts to go sideways in the foam, move up to one side and push it straight again.

When you get waist deep, hop on the trampoline and drop your rudders. If the water is too shallow for the rudders, just drop them as far as they will go—you need steerage way at this point. If the rudders are not down all the way, remember that you will have a lot of tiller load and will need to put some muscle into steering. The critical thing here is to keep your cat moving. If you let it round into the wind, you'll come to a quick stop which will put you at the mercy of the waves. If you have centerboards, don't put them down more than six inches until you're through the surfline. Otherwise, you could seriously damage your hulls if you get pushed backwards and land back on the beach.

When your rudders are down and you have the tiller, sheet in to pick up speed. Once you get moving, angle off a little for more speed and move your weight forward a little as you go over waves. If a wave breaks in front of you, just concentrate on keeping your speed up. As the wave hits, move forward and steer straight into the wave. You may need to backwind your sails or scull your rudders to get back on course after the wave has passed. Remember, your main concern is keeping your speed up. As long as you are moving well you're safe since the waves can't carry you up and over backwards and can't turn you sideways. Practice sailing out through surf in the small stuff at first—leave the big waves for later.

HINTS FOR SAILING OUT THROUGH SURF

1. Don't sail through large waves unless the wind is blowing parallel to the beach or strongly offshore.
2. Don't get sideways in the surf. If you do, get your cat headed straight into the waves as soon as possible.
3. Keep moving at top speed. Concentrate and adjust your sails to the tell-tails and masthead or bridle fly.
4. Steer into breaking waves and move your weight forward to help your cat over them. Hanging onto the forward crossbar is a good way to stay aboard as the wave washes past you.

In a strong sideshore breeze, pounding out through small surf is easy so long as you keep your cat driving fast.

CAPSIZING IN THE SURF

There are two things to consider if you capsize in the surf: yourself and your boat, in that order. Most of the time you can work on getting your cat righted. Remember that you don't want to get between your cat and the shore, since another wave could easily push your cat on top of you.

In small surf under three feet, get your righting line out and try and bring your cat on her feet again (chapter 8). If things aren't going well, remember to keep the bows heading into the waves. Swim them around if you have to, but get them pointed towards the surf—this will greatly increase your chances of getting your cat to the beach without damage.

In large or consistent medium surf (three feet and over), the risk of getting hurt is much greater. If you can't right your cat quickly in such conditions, or it's really moving around in the surf, the smartest thing to do is get out of the way. You may end up with a broken cat, but at least you'll be in shape to fix it and sail again! Again, common sense should dictate your efforts in trying to right your cat in marginal conditions. It's no fun to watch your cat getting beat up in the surf, but hopefully you can see the forces involved and be able to judge whether you can handle them or not.

PART III

SAFETY, MAINTENANCE AND TRANSPORT

15/
SAFETY

While dismasting, capsizing and man overboard were gone over in chapter eight, there are still other safety factors to consider such as rig check, weather check, electrocution, ex-

posure, life jackets, and the dangers of offshore sailing. Chances are that help is close by when something happens, especially in a harbor. But good cat sailors rarely need any help since they use common sense, keep their cats in good shape, and have an almost sixth sense about being able to detect trouble before it happens. For starters, a good cat sailor avoids breakdowns by going over his rigging often.

RIG RIGHT, RIG TIGHT

Before you go sailing make a quick check of your rigging. Look for signs of wear on the lines and shrouds, make sure all your shackles are tight, and make sure cotter keys and rings are in place.

Simple items like hull plugs can make for embarrassing situations if they're forgotten. It's also a good idea to carry some extra shackles and a few tools on board.

LIFE JACKETS

Never leave shore without a lifejacket. If you or your crew can't swim very well, wear one all the time. All it takes to go overboard is an accidental jibe or the unexpected motion of a big wave.

WEATHER CHECK

It's a good idea to check the weather report before going out, particularly if you're planning to sail offshore. A sudden weather change could turn a pleasant afternoon sail into a fight for survival. You can get information on the weather from newspapers, special weather frequencies on the radio, and from harbor departments. Many areas have a phone number for a continuous weather report.

ELECTROCUTION

Most catamaran masts are aluminum—a material that conducts electricity very well. The danger, of course, is that your mast will hit an overhead wire while you are hanging onto your cat. This has killed several sailors while they were moving their cats around in storage and launching areas. Others have been electrocuted by sailing into a wire which crossed a lake or river.

Electrical storms are also a danger. If you see one approaching, go for the beach. If you end up in the middle of one, the safest thing to do is capsize your cat and sit on a hull until the danger passes.

OFFSHORE WINDS

Many cat sailors have sailed out to sea in an offshore wind and were never seen again. If you go out in this situation, you'd

SAFETY, MAINTENANCE
AND TRANSPORT

better be good at sailing your cat to weather (chapter 8). This is especially true if it's really blowing. The ride out to sea is easy and fun, but coming back to shore against the wind can be a real workout.

EXPOSURE

One of the most underrated dangers of sailing is exposure. Cold water and air can easily drain your strength. It is imperative to have adequate weather gear when you're sailing in cold conditions. Many sailors use wetsuits, others use foul weather gear. Even if the weather looks good, take the gear along if there is the slightest chance of change. If you're sailing in an area where the water is really cold, don't sail too far from possible help. Areas such as Lake Tahoe claim victims every year. Typically, a sailor will go out on a nice warm morning in light air. By the afternoon, he's far from shore when the wind begins to whistle and the waves pick up. Fatigue sets in, and if he capsizes, his chances for survival are very slim. Even with a wetsuit, exposure is a real danger if you're far away from help.

DROWNING

A potential danger with boats that can capsize is getting caught under the boat after it goes over. On cats, this is very unlikely except with persons using a trapeze. Sometimes the harness hooks onto something during a capsize. It's a smart idea to carry a knife or a small pair of wire cutters if you're using a trapeze. New trapeze harnesses have reduced this problem. These harnesses have safety hooks which unclip. One step better is a new harness that is called a "no hook" harness which eliminates the danger completely.

NEVER LEAVE YOUR CAT

The greatest danger of drowning occurs when people leave their overturned boats. Many people have drowned while trying to swim to shore after their boat has capsized. Regardless of what happens, stay with your cat if it's dismasted, capsized, whatever. A cat, capsized or rightside up, makes a great platform. It won't sink, so you're practically guaranteed rescue if you stay with it.

16/
MAINTENANCE

The modern fiberglass catamaran is relatively maintenance free. But without some routine care trouble can develop and your cat's resale value can be reduced considerably. Keeping your cat in tip-top shape requires an understanding of cleaning agents, fiberglass repair, and sail maintenance.

SAIL CARE

Today's sails are made of synthetic materials called Dacron, Kevlar or Mylar. Unlike canvas sails of years ago, these fabrics resist rotting and, with proper care, can last years longer. But like fiberglass, these fabrics need some care:

1. Don't let your sails flutter on the beach. Rapid fluttering or whipping breaks down the fiber in the sailcloth and tears up the thread that holds the sail together. If you leave your cat rigged up for a while, either backwind the sails or take them down.

2. Be careful with zipper-luffed jibs. Zippers can be ruined by being forced onto the forestay. Hoist a zippered jib by feeding it onto the forestay with one hand while you pull the halyard with your other hand. If you're on a beach be especially conscious of keeping

the jib out of the sand. Sand can really mess up the zipper.

3. If you do leave your cat with the sail up, turn it into the wind and let off the downhaul on the mainsail. Turning your cat into the wind will keep the sail from chafing on the shrouds.

4. When dropping your mainsail, make sure you have control of it as the luff comes out of the mast. A sail that gets away from you in a lot of wind will probably end up with broken battens.

5. Folding your sails puts sharp creases in them. Roll them up instead (chapter 7). And before you roll your sails up, ease the batten tension on them so they won't stretch unnecessarily.

6. If you capsize, try to keep from falling on the sails as they lie in the water.

7. The enemies of high-tech sail fibers are sun, salt, and

sand. Rinsing your sails with fresh water and drying them out can add years of life to them.

8. Oil, grease and rust spots are things you have to live with. Sails don't clean up very well, and chemicals that remove rust spots and grease will also eat up the material. If you do wash your sails, never put them in a washing machine. Instead lay them out on a lawn or a clean cement surface and hose them down. Using a light detergent, scrub them with a soft brush taking care not to tear up the threads. After washing, make sure your sails are completely dry before storing them away.

9. Give your sails an inspection every few months for signs of wear. Chafed threads, missing batten pocket ends, broken battens, loose rivets, and small holes or tears should be repaired as soon as they are spotted.

10. Good preventative measures are needed to prevent chafe. Tape spreader tips and other areas of the rigging that could possibly puncture a sail. Plastic shroud covers are also a good idea; they reduce abrasion between the sails and the shrouds.

11. Always keeping your sails out of the sun whenever possible is probably the best favor you can do for them. The sun's rays are very damaging to Dacron fiber.

12. The best way to keep your sails clean is to keep your rigging clean. Wash down your mast, halyards, and stays regularly with a sponge and soapy water.

RIGGING

Keep an eye on your shrouds and stays for broken wire strands or kinks. If the swedge fittings at the ends of the shrouds show any cracks, replace them—this will prevent a dismasting.

Plastic covers on your shrouds can also discourage rust and make cleaning easier. Bright Boy or other metal cleaners are ideal for keeping wire rigging rust-free.

CHAINPLATES

Chainplates on Hobie 14's and other cats should be inspected for any sign of working loose or corrosion, especially if you sail

in salt water. Corroded chainplates should be replaced. Sometimes, if the corrosion has gone too far, relocating the chainplates is necessary. New chainplates can be riveted to a new
location either just forward or aft of the original chainplate positions. The holes left from the old chainplates can be filled with

silicone sealer or a similar product. Chain plate corrosion can be lessened with plastic chain plate covers.

RUDDER ASSEMBLY

1. Rudder pins are subject to a lot of strain and should be checked for wear or bend.
2. All nicks, chips, and cracks in your rudders or centerboards can lead to breakage. Repairs can be made by using Marine Tex or a similar filler product.
3. Rudder gudgeons can and do crack—keep an eye on them for fatigue.
4. Corrosion can develop between the tiller extension and the tiller crossbar. Shims can be placed inside the tiller crossbar if corrosion loosens the assembly. But if the corrosion becomes too bad, the entire bar may have to be replaced.
5. Sometimes the automatic kick-up rudder systems on Hobie Cats can be a source of trouble, either kicking up too easily or being too stiff. Underneath each rudder casting is a teflon screw that will usually solve the problem. Tighten the screws and you will increase the locking power. Loosening them will allow your rudders to kick up easier. These screws can be tough to turn, so have some spray lubricant and a large flathead screwdriver on hand for this adjustment.

TRAMPOLINE CARE

1. Inspect trampoline lacings for wear. If the lacings are frayed re-string your trampoline with new cord. Some sailors like to use shock cord for lacing because it distributes the load evenly and helps keep the trampoline tight.
2. Check the trampoline grommets for wearing or tearing. A sailmaker can repair a popped or torn-away grommet. Rolled-edge spur grommets are the best kind to use for these repairs since the grommets won't tear into the trampoline.
3. Periodically wash the trampoline with a light detergent and a soft brush. Your trampoline will also last longer if it's washed down with fresh water after sailing.

ALUMINUM

Salt water gets into everything, including anodized aluminum masts and booms. Here is a tip for spar care:

1. Rinse your spars off with fresh water after each sail. If you spot some corrosion, clean the affected area with "Bright Boy" or some other metal cleaner. Once your spars are clean, try waxing them for maximum protection.

FIBERGLASS CARE

Fiberglass hulls are very durable and require little care. However, it's wise not to leave your boat in the water for more than two days. Otherwise, hull fading begins. The sun also causes fading, especially with colored hulls in red or blue. If you keep your cat outdoors, covers are a good idea if you want those bright colors to remain that way (figure 1). A good wax helps protect the hulls also, but waxing your hulls will slow your cat down slightly, since it beads up water and creates air pockets along the hulls when you're sailing. This is one of the reasons why daysailors usually care for their hulls in a different way than racers do.

DAYSAILER HULL CARE

1. Wash off your hulls after every sail.
2. Keep your cat covered.

Figure 1

3. If your hulls begin to fade try buffing them back into condition:
   a. First, wipe the entire fiberglass surface with a cloth saturated with acetone.
   b. Apply buffing compound to a buffer and polish the hulls, holding the buffer at a 45 degree angle to the surfaces. The deeper the fading the grittier the compound you need. But be careful of applying too much pressure with the buffer—you can take the gel coat off.
4. Deep scratches can be removed by using number 400 or 600 wet-dry sandpaper. After sanding, buff the area to bring back the gloss.
5. After the hulls are buffed and the scratches removed, give them two coats of wax. Even better than waxing is using one of the new amino functional products (such as Fas Glas) for maximum protection.

RACER HULL CARE

1. Always wash down with fresh water after sailing.
2. Keep the hulls free of all scratches.
3. While buffing the hulls is o.k., don't wax them. Waxed hulls are slower than ones without wax.
4. Before a regatta, wet sand the hulls with number 600 wet-dry paper and clean them off with a light detergent.
5. Don't store your cat outdoors if you want to keep it looking its best.

COMMON LEAK REPAIR

Most leaks in your hulls are not caused by hull cracks or seam openings and therefore can be easily repaired. If your hulls are collecting water, first try re-sealing all the fittings. Remove all screws and fasteners that are attached to the hulls. Then clean the open areas with acetone and let them dry completely. After cleaning, re-seal each screw and fitting with clear silicone and then re-assemble your cat.

If your hulls still leak after a re-sealing, you may have cracks in your hull-to-deck seams. Hobie and Prindle cats are sometimes plagued with this problem. For crack repair, do the following:

1. Chip away all loose glue and resin from the seams.
2. Clean the entire lip surrounding the hulls with acetone.
3. Turn your cat upside down and check for water that may have been trapped inside the hulls. If water seeps through a cracked area, drain your cat until dry.
4. With a mixture of laminating resin and catalyst, fill the cracks. Dripping the mixture from a small can is often the best way to fill. If the cracks are wide, you may need clamps to close the areas up.
5. Once the resin has dried, sand the repaired areas smooth.

DINGS AND SUCH

Sooner or later you'll get a ding on one of your hulls. If you keep your cat on a beach, your hulls will get worn from being dragged across the sand. So it's a good idea to be familiar with fiberglass repair.

Fiberglass is not difficult to work with. A good book on fiberglass repair for the beginner is *Fiberglass Repair* by Paul Tetricks (Cornell Maritime Press Inc., Cambridge). But even without a book, the basics of repair are easy. Small punctures can be filled with Bondo, Hobie Stuff, Dynaglass, Marine Tex, etc. Once filled with one of these epoxy fillers, the punctured area should be sanded smooth and then sprayed with color-matching gel coat.

To rebuild keels, lay sheets of fiberglass cloth on top of each other until the keels are slightly deeper than they were originally. After glassing, sand them down until the original shapes are restored.

GEL COAT

Gel coat is the color finish on fiberglass. It is sprayed inside the hull and deck molds as a cat is being built. For applying new gel coat to an area, do the following:

SURFACE PREPARATION
1. Sand the area to be sprayed with 180 grit sandpaper and lightly sand the surrounding area with 600 paper. Any unfare surfaces should be filled and fared perfectly before gel coat is applied.

2. After the final sanding, clean the surface and mask off the area to protect the rest of your boat from overspray.

MIXTURE AND APPLICATION

First, thin the gel coat with polyester 944-W-841 acetone. Use four parts of gel coat to one part of acetone. Next, add the catalyst. About 10 to 15 cc. per quart will work well depending upon the temperature. After your sprayer is filled, adjust the air pressure to between 40 and 60 pounds.

The first spraying (first coat) should be a very light one. Let the first coat dry one to three minutes. Follow with a heavier coat, being careful not to spray outside the area of the first coat, since you don't want to build up a noticeable edge.

Remember that gel coat is very air sensitive and that the outer skin will not completely harden unless it's sealed off. The best way to seal off gel coat is to spray a thin poly-vinyl alcohol coating over the gel coat. Called Ram Plastilease 512-B, the poly-vinyl alcohol (P VA) should be applied after the final gel coat layer is applied and has air-dried for five to fifteen minutes (or until tacky to the touch.)

Another method for gel coat cure is to add a surfacing agent such as Ram Surfacing Agent 85-X3 to the gel coat mixture. Use about 5 cc per quart, mix it completely into the thinned gel coat as it begins to harden. This forms an effective air sealing film.

Allow the gel coat to cure (from 2 to 24 hours) after spraying. Cure time depends on air temperature, humidity, and the acetone-catalyst mixture that was used. A warmer temperature shortens cure time.

While gel coat is best for repairs, if you want to re-do your hulls entirely, painting is best. Applying new gel coat to an entire cat is expensive and it adds unnecessary weight. Painting the hulls and decks with a product like Dupont Emerone is much better. Paint is lighter, tougher, and thinner, and it can also be applied by any auto paint shop.

17/
TRANSPORT

Trailers have always been a source of aggravation to the traveling catamaran racer. It seems your trailer is always rusting, falling apart, or having tail light problems. While a cat sailor may spend hours detailing his beloved cat, chances are his trailer sorely needs a paint job.

When a new cat sailor buys his cat, he may spend over his budget on expensive extras but will get the cheapest trailer available. The problem here is that even the hottest looking cat can't get to a regatta if its cheap neglected trailer breaks down in the middle of nowhere. Buying a good trailer and taking care of it will save you a lot of grief down the road.

TIPS FOR TRAILER BUYING

1. Springs. Your trailer must have springs that can adequately handle the load of your cat and the extra gear you pile on top of it. If the springs don't take the shock of a bumpy road, your cat will.

2. Wheels. Sturdy 12-inch wheels are the best for long distance trailering. Eight-inch wheels can quickly burn out bearings. Eight-inch wheels can usually be replaced with 12-inchers, but you may experience

some problems with the fenders. Also, keep a spare tire with you.

3. Bearings. You'll need good grease seals if you plan to launch your cat at a ramp where the wheels will be submerged. Sealed pressure grease caps (Buddy Bearings) are the best.

4. Balance. Balancing the trailer load is very important. Balance is a function of load and axle placement. A load too far forward will cause the rear of your car to squat, which is rough on your car's back tires. A forward load also increases your trailer's tendency to flex. A load too far back causes the trailer to weave. The properly loaded trailer has 40 to 60 percent of the weight forward. If your trailer itself is unbalanced, the axles can be modified to solve the problem.

5. Construction. Trailers are made of aluminum or steel. Aluminum trailers are more expensive, but they are much better than the steel ones since they are lighter and are not as susceptible to rust and corrosion. Steel

SAFETY, MAINTENANCE
AND TRANSPORT

trailers will rust quickly if they are not galvanized or kept well painted. For sheer durability, galvanized trailers are the best.

6. Lights. Lighting is usually the main source of headaches for the trailer sailor. Lights are either so cheap they don't work, or they are illegal as far as your state code is concerned. Always make sure you're buying a trailer that has a top-notch lighting system—it's well worth it. Your lights must meet the minimum requirements that your state's Department of Motor Vehicles has established.

7. Hitches. Purchase a strong hitch. A super trailer isn't worth much if it's overturned on a highway with your cat under it. Trailer hitches come in a variety of shapes and sizes. Most cat trailers connect to a ball hitch that is bolted or welded to the underbody of the towing vehicle. Some hitches are made to clamp onto the rear bumper, but these are bad for your car. The best hitch is a heavy duty equalizing hitch. You can get away with a cheaper hitch though, since cats are so light. Just make sure the ball size complements your trailer's coupler. A ball that is too small may allow your trailer to take off on its own down the highway. The standard ball for most trailers is 1⅞ inches.

A good trailer will have a safety lock that will prevent your trailer from getting away from you no matter what happens. But you should still hook up the safety chain.

SECURING TO THE TRAILER

It's pretty easy to imagine what can happen to a cat that is not tied securely to its trailer. A cat that flies off its trailer at 60 mph will not only be totally destroyed, but it just might kill someone, too. Always take the time to tie your cat securely to its trailer. Here's the way to do it right:

1. Place your cat on the trailer so the tongue weight is moderate. A moderate tongue weight should allow you to lift the tongue end of the trailer with little effort. But if you can lift it with just a finger, then your cat is too far aft.

2. Drop the mast and make sure that it extends no more

than three feet beyond the taillight assembly. If it extends past three feet, a red flag must be tied on the end.

3. Coil all wires and lines and secure them to the trampoline or mast (figure 1). After the wires and lines are made up and secured, place some padding under the mast and tie it to both the aft crossbar (figure 2) and the forward mast crutch.

Figure 1

Figure 2

SAFETY, MAINTENANCE
AND TRANSPORT

4. Tie down the entire rudder assembly with two pieces of line port and starboard, wrapping around the tiller crossbar and the aft crossbar. If you're going a long distance, it's best to remove the rudders entirely.
5. Tie down the cat to the trailer with trucker's hitches or a leverage sheepshank (figure 3). Your cat should be tied fore and aft and laterally. A well-tied cat cannot move forward, aft, or sideways on its trailer (figure 4).

Figure 3

LEVERAGE SHEEPSHANK

Figure 4

THINGS TO REMEMBER

1. You must drive differently with a trailer behind you. The heavier the rig, the more time you'll need for stopping and accelerating.
2. A car with a small engine will really be working while towing. Keep an eye on engine temperature, transmission fluid level, and the brake system. And keep your tires properly inflated.
3. Visibility is restricted. Extended side mirrors are often needed.
4. You've got a wide load behind you. Remember this when turning and passing.
5. For long distance trips, take off the trampoline. This will decrease windage and will reduce the chances of your rig giving you trouble in a lot of wind.

LIGHTING

Figure 5

If your lighting is giving you a problem, use the schematic below for correcting it (figure 5). The schematic applies to most American cars. For foreign cars, you can get a conversion kit that will get you lit up legally.

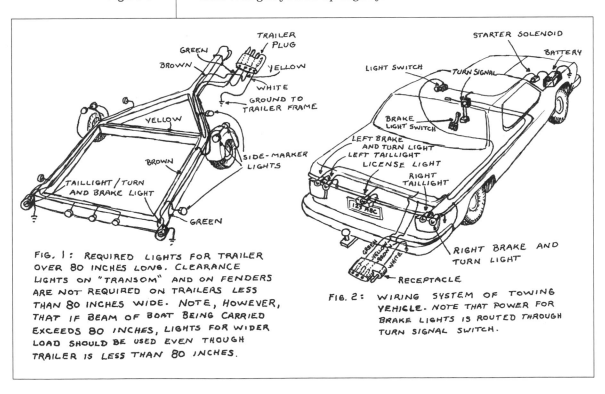

FIG. 1: REQUIRED LIGHTS FOR TRAILER OVER 80 INCHES LONG. CLEARANCE LIGHTS ON "TRANSOM" AND ON FENDERS ARE NOT REQUIRED ON TRAILERS LESS THAN 80 INCHES WIDE. NOTE, HOWEVER, THAT IF BEAM OF BOAT BEING CARRIED EXCEEDS 80 INCHES, LIGHTS FOR WIDER LOAD SHOULD BE USED EVEN THOUGH TRAILER IS LESS THAN 80 INCHES.

FIG. 2: WIRING SYSTEM OF TOWING VEHICLE. NOTE THAT POWER FOR BRAKE LIGHTS IS ROUTED THROUGH TURN SIGNAL SWITCH.

SAFETY, MAINTENANCE
AND TRANSPORT

GENERAL TRAILER MAINTENANCE

1. The easiest thing you can do that can often make the biggest difference in mileage is to check your tire inflation.
2. Check the grease levels in your bearings once in a while. If your wheels begin to make some rough sounding noises, you probably need to replace the bearings.
3. If you pull your trailer out of salt water, try and get it sprayed down with fresh water as soon as possible. Paint any rusting surfaces right away—rust is your trailer's greatest enemy.
4. Keep all the nuts on your trailer tightened up—they have a way of working loose after a few trips.
5. Keep an eye out for cracks on trailers that are primarily welded together—trailers do a lot of flexing.
6. The mast supports on many trailers tend to sway side to side—you may want to have extra support arms welded on if your mast support looks marginal.
7. Grease and clean the rollers regularly so they roll smoothly. Stiff rollers will smudge the hulls of your cat.
8. Keep a spare trailer tire and the tools to change it.

GLOSSARY

A

ABACK—A sail pushed back by the wind, so that it slows the forward motion of a cat. (A jib purposely trimmed to windward is backwinded, not aback).

ABAFT—A trem used to describe the relative position of an object that is farther aft than some other point of reference. The mainsheet is abaft the mast, for example.

ABEAM—A position reference. Any object bearing at right angles to a cats keel line is abeam.

AERODYNAMIC FORCE—The total energy produced by the cats sails through a deviation of the airflow.

AFT—A position reference toward a boat's stern.

ALEE—To the side opposite from which the wind is blowing.

AMIDSHIP—Between bow and stern, the middle of the cat. Also, between her port and starboard sides.

APPARENT WIND—The vector (change in direction) produced by a cat's forward speed. The wind one experiences on a moving cat.

ASPECT RATIO—The relationship between a horizontal and vertical dimension. A tall mast and short boom make a high aspect ratio sail plan.

B

BACKING—A change in wind direction counter-clockwise in relation to a compass.

BACKWIND—Wind deflected from a forward sail onto the sail behind it.

BACKWINDING—Holding a cat's sail out the windward side to assist in turning. Leaving another cat's disturbed air.

BARBER HAULER—A device similar to a traveler in that it is used for the athwartships adjustment of jibsheets.

BARGING—Approaching a starting line, in order to start, from a position to windward of the lay line to the end of the line.

BATTEN—A thin, narrow strip of wood or fiberglass used to stiffen up the shape of a cat sail.

BEAM—(1) The width of a hull or hulls. (2) At right angles to the centerline of the cat.

BEAR—To change direction; to bear up is to turn into the wind; to bear off to turn away from the wind.

BEATING—Tacking the cat back and forth to gain distance in a windward direction.

BECKET—A "U"- shaped piece of metal which a block or line is attached to.

BEFORE THE WIND—Sailing with the wind from astern—in the same direction toward which the wind is blowing.

BERNOULIS PRINCIPLE—If the velocity of the air flowing past one side of an air-foil is greater than that on the other side, the pressure correspondingly decreases on the former side creating a suction like that which creates the lift of an airplane wing and the pull of a cat's sail.

BOLT ROPE—Reinforcing rope sewn on the luff and foot of a sail.

BOOM—Pole or spar attached to the mast to which the foot (lower edge) of a sail is fastened.

BOOM VANG—A block and tackle system, normally connected at mid boom, and from there to the mast base. It pulls down and flattens the mainsail's luff as well as keeps its leech from sagging off, used only on offwind legs.

BOW—The forward part of a cat's hulls.

BRIDLE VANE—A wind indicator placed near the forestay adjuster between the bows.

BRIDLE WIRE—A wire which comes up from a cat's bow to meet and support its forestay.

BROAD REACHING—Sailing with the wind aft of abeam.

BY THE LEE—Sailing downwind at an angle greater than 180 degrees to the true wind (watch for the accidental jibe).

C

CAMBER—The concavity of the curve of an airfoil.

CAPSIZE—To turn the cat over on her side.

CASTOFF—To let go.

CATBOAT—A single-masted boat that does not carry a sail before the mast.

CENTERBOARD—A movable plate generally made of fiberglass that can be raised or lowered through the keels of a cat's hulls. The centerboard imparts stability and helps to prevent leeway.

CHAFE—To wear the surface of a sail, rigging or spar by rubbing.

CHAINPLATES—Metal strips fastened to the sides of a boat to which shrouds are attached.

CHOP—Short irregular waves.

CLEAR AIR—Air flow undisturbed by the presence of other cats or boats.

CLEAT—A horned fitting in wood or metal to which lines are made fast.

CLEW—The lower aft corner of a sail.

CLOSEHAULED—Sailing close to the wind.

COLLISION COURSE—If the relative bearing of the two boats converging doesn't change, eventually they will collide.

COMING ABOUT—Bringing the cat from one tack to another when sailing upwind.

CREST—The top of a wave.

D

DAGGERBOARD—A removable unpivoted keel.

DEAD DOWNWIND—Directly to leeward.

DECK—The covered part of the top of a cat.

DIRTY AIR—1. The deviated, confused air flow astern and to leeward of a competitor. 2. Backwind or blanket.

DOG BOAT—A slow, or very beat up cat.

DOLPHIN STRIKER—A wire or rod which runs across a cat's beam that attaches to the underside of her forward crossbar to help support the mast.

DOWNHAUL—1. A fitting or control line at the tack of a sail that tightens the luff. 2. A control line to pull down the main boom on its gooseneck slide.

DOWNWIND—Opposite to the wind direction, to leeward.

DRAFT—The degree of concavity.

DRAG—1. Resistance caused by a hull shape in a fluid medium. 2. Resistance caused by an airfoil in an atmospheric medium.

DRIVE—To sail hard at a lower instead of higher angle to the wind when beating. Footing.

E

EASE OFF—1. To slacken sheets. 2. To fall off the wind by pulling the tiller.

EYE OF THE WIND—The exact direction from which the true wind is coming.

F

FAIRLEADS—Small, smooth fittings through which a line passes, changing its direction.

FALL OFF—To alter course away from the wind.

FAVORED END—1. The upwind end of a starting line for starting. 2. The downwind end of a starting line for finishing.

FETCH—When sailors can reach the place they are sailing to without tacking.

FITTING—An item of marine hardware.

FLAT SAIL—1. Minimum draft in a sail, the opposite of a full sail.

FOOT—1. The bottom edge of a sail, extending from tack to clew. 2. To sail hard at a low heading when going upwind.

FORE AND AFT—In the direction of the keel(s).

FORESTAY—A wire mast support leading forward to the bridle wires which come up from each bow.

FREE TO TACK—The ability of a cat to tack without interfering with a competitor.

FULL SAIL—A sail with a good amount of draft, the opposite of a flat sail.

FURL—1. To roll and tie a sail on a boom. 2. To roll a jib up on a headstay.

G

GEL COAT—The sprayed on color finish which coats a fiberglass hull.

GOOSENECK—Fitting connecting the boom to the mast.

GROMMET—A metal ring set into material for a line to attach to or through.

GROOVE—To find the fastest sailing method for a given wind, sea or heading.

GUDGEONS—Fittings mounted on the stern of a cat's hulls to which the rudders are attached.

GUST—A sudden increase in wind velocity.

GYBE—I. Same as jibe. 2. Complete a change of tack with the leech of a sail passing through the eye of the wind.

H

HALYARD—A wire or rope used to hoist a sail.

HANK(S)—Clip(s) fastened onto the luff of a jib for attaching it to the forestay.

HAUL—To pull in.

HEAD—The top of a sail.

HEADED TACK—The tack that is affected by a header, which forces a cat to point away from the median wind.

HEADER—A change in wind direction towards the bow of a cat.

HEADING—The direction in which a cat is traveling.

HEADSTAY—1. The forward wire supporting the mast. 2. Forestay.

HEAD TO WIND—In irons; or pointed with bows directly into the wind with sails luffing.

HEAD UP—To alter course toward the wind.

HEEL—Sideways deviation from the vertical; to tip.

HELM—Tiller which controls rudders.

HIKE—To climb out on the windward side; to trapeze.

HOBBY HORSE—To sail with the bows and sterns rising and falling in a regular pattern.

HOIST—To pull up.

I

INBOARD—1. Within the hull. 2. To move from a hiked position back toward the trampoline or deck.

INDUCED DRAG—Drag caused by eddies along the foot and head of a sail.

IN IRONS—State of a cat which is stationary, pointing directly into the wind and temporarily unable to turn in either direction.

INSIDE—Between a competitor and a mark or the rhumb line.

J

JAM CLEAT—A device which enables one to make fast a sheet without having to tie a knot.

L

LAYLINE—The course that permits a close-hauled cat or a cat sailing on an optimal angle on the run (90 apparent wind) to just clear the mark in the existing breeze.

LEADING EDGE—The foremost edge of a sail.

LEECH—The after edge of a sail.

LEE HELM—Tendency of a cat to turn itself away from the wind.

LEEWARD—The side away from the wind.

LEEWARD MARK—The mark that terminates the second reach and/or the run that initiates the second or third beat.

LEEWAY—Cat's sideways drift due to wind pressure.

LIFT—A change in wind direction allowing a cat to point higher, or ease sails without changing course.

LIFTED TACK—1. The tack that carries a close-hauled cat closer to the next mark. 2. The tack that carries a running cat away from the next mark.

LOOSE FOOTED—A mainsail not held to a boom its entire length.

LUFF—I . Leading edge of a sail. 2. The flogging of sails due to improper trim or heading.

LUFF ROPE—The rope sewed to the luff of a sail.

LUFF TENSION—The pressure exerted on a sail's luff by a down-haul or Cunningham to adjust the location of its draft.

LUFF UP—To alter course so that the cat is sailing at a narrower angle to the wind.

LULL—A brief dying of the air.

M

MAINSAIL—A sail set aft of a mast.

MAINSHEET—A line that controls the angle of the mainsail in its relation to the wind.

MARK—Usual term for a buoy or other object used as a turning point in a course for racing.

MAST—A vertical spar supporting a boom and sails.

MAST RAKE—Positioning the top of the mast fore or aft in relation to the straight up and down position.

O

OFF THE WIND—1. Sailing at a wide angle to the wind. 2. Reaching or running.

ON THE WIND—1. Sailing at a narrow angle to the wind. 2. Pointing, beating, sailing closehauled and sailing to weather.

ONE DESIGN—An organized class of identical racing boats.

ONE-LEG-BEAT—A windward leg the major portion of which is sailed on one tack.

OSCILLATING WIND—A windshift that will be followed by a shift to the original direction, or past it, prior to the completion of a leg.

OUTHAUL—A line that holds the mainsail's clew to the boom and adjusts its foot tension.

OUTSIDE—Beyond a competitor that is nearer the mark or the rhumbline.

OVERSTANDING—Choosing an approach tack that clears the mark by a greater distance than necessary, consequent to sailing beyond the layline.

P

PAINTER—Line tied to the bow of a boat.

PAY OUT—To slacken a sheet.

PEARL—To stick a bow in under the surface of the water.

PERSISTENT WIND—A shift in wind direction that is not followed by a return to the original direction prior to the completion of a leg.

PINCHING—When sailing close-hauled with the luff of the sail slack; too close to the wind.

PINTLE—Part of the mounting for the rudder at the back of a cat which fits into the gudgeon.

PITCHING—Fore and aft oscillation of the hulls; hobby horsing.

PITCHPOLE—To flip over from an irreversible pearl

POINTING—Sailing close to the wind.

PORT SIDE—The left side of a boat facing forward.

PORT TACK—Wind coming from the port side.

PUFF—A sudden burst of wind that is blowing stronger than what is blowing at the time.

PYLONS—Metal posts which rise from a hull to support a trampoline frame.

R

RAKE—The angle of a boat's mast from vertical.

REACHING—When a boat sails with the wind abeam or slightly forward or aft of the beam.

REEFING—Reducing area of a sail by partly lowering and securing it.

RHUMBLINE—The straightline course between one mark and the next.

RIG—Mast, sails and various lines used in connection with them.

ROCKER—Downward curve of the hull, its amount of bow and stern lift.

ROLLER FURLING JIB—A mechanical system for rolling the jib around its own luff wire.

ROUNDING UP—The action of the boat as it turns toward the wind.

RUDDER—Device(s) fastened vertically at the stern(s) which directs the course of a boat.

RUNNING—When a boat sails dead before the wind.

RUNNING RIGGING—Halyards, sheets and all movable rigging.

S

SAILING CIRCLE—An imaginary circle which shows where a boat can sail in respect to the true wind.

SCULLING—Moving the tiller back and forth quickly to move the boat ahead.

SHACKLE—Universal device for attaching sails, sheets, rigging, etc., consisting of a 'U' shape with a removable bolt.

SHEET—Rope controlling the angle of a sail.

SHIFT—A change of wind direction.

SHROUD—Sidestay; wire that holds mast up on two sides.

SIDESLIP—Drifting downwind at the cost of making headway upwind.

SLACK—To ease or pay out a sheet.

SLOOP—Type of sailing boat with fore-and-aft mainsail and one jib set on a single mast.

SLOT EFFECT—The funneling of air behind the mainsail through the slot formed between the main and jib. This increases the velocity of the air on the lee side of the main thereby increasing its suction and efficiency.

SPARS—Mast and boom.

SPREADER—Strut projecting from the side of the mast to brace the stays or diamond wires.

SQUALL—A sudden and violent gust of wind often accompanied by rain, snow and lightning.

STALL—A breakdown of aerodynamic forces, usually caused by separation of air flow on the leeward side of a sail.

STANDING RIGGING—All wires supporting the mast.

STARBOARD—Right side, when facing forward.

STARBOARD TACK—State of a boat when it is sailing with the wind on the starboard side.

STAY—Wire supporting the mast.

STEP—1. Point of the deck or bottom of the boat where the base of the mast rests. 2. To erect the mast.

STERN—Back of a hull(s).

STRATEGY—A weather leg and starting plan formulated prior to a start of a race.

SURF—1. To sail at high speed down the face of a wave. 2. To sail up the face of a wave when leaving a shore.

SYMMETRICAL HULL—A hull which is curved evenly on both sides.

T

TACK—1. To sail a zig-zag course in the direction from which the wind is blowing. 2. Lower forward corner of a sail.

TACTICS—The means by which a given race is fought.

TANG—Fitting on mast which shrouds are connected to.

TAUT—With no slack, set very tight.

TELL-TALE—Short pieces of ribbon or yarn attached to sails or shrouds to help a sailor read the wind.

THWARTSHIPS—At right angles to the fore and aft line.

TILLER—Device which controls rudder; same as helm.

TRAMPOLINE—Canvas deck on a cat which extends from side to side across its beam.

TRANSOM—Stern end of cat where rudders are attached to gudgeons.

TRAPEZE—A device used to put bodies out from the weather rail to deter heel.

TRAVELER—Metal rod which runs across a cat's beam to which main or jib blocks and cleats are attached.

TRIM—To adjust sheet tension.

TROUGH—The hollow between two waves.

TRUE WIND—The wind that would be present in the absence of a moving boat.

TURNBUCKLES—A coupling threaded so that it may be shortened or extended.

TWO-BLOCKED—When the two blocks of a tackle have been drawn together as close as possible.

U

UNA RIG—A cat powered only by a mainsail.

UPWIND—Toward the wind.

V

VANG—A line or block system used to hold the boom down. Used primarily for offwind sailing.

VEERING—A change in wind direction counterclockwise in relation to a compass.

W

WAKE—V-shaped pattern of waves made in water behind a moving boat.

WAY—Momentum.

WEATHER—Side of an object facing the wind.

WETTED SURFACE—Area of a cat's hulls in contact with the water.

WIND SHIFT—Change of wind direction.

WINDWARD—Facing the wind, upwind.

KNOTS

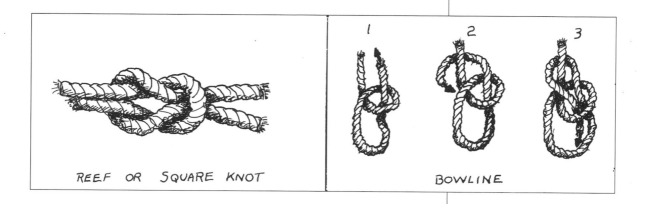

REEF OR SQUARE KNOT

1 2 3

BOWLINE

FIGURE EIGHT KNOT

TWO HALF HITCHES

CLEAT HALF HITCH

APPENDIX

CATAMARAN MAGAZINES

Hobie Hotline
P.O. Box 1008
Oceanside, California 92054

Catamaran Sailor
P.O. Box 2060
Key Largo, Florida 33037

Prindle Letter
1801 East Borchard Ave.
Santa Ana, California 92705

Multihulls
421 Hancock Street
North Quincy, Massachusetts
    02171

MAJOR CATAMARAN MANUFACTURERS

Hobie Cat Company
4925 Oceanside Blvd.
Oceanside, California 92056
760-758-9100

NACRA and PRINDLE
    CATAMARANS
Performance Sailcraft
1801 E. Borchard Avenue
Santa Ana, CA 92705
714-541-6643

G-Force Multihulls
G-Cat beach Catamarans
7100 142nd Avenue North
Largo, FL 33771
813-536-4114

Mystere Catamarans
Mystere International
15027th Avenue
Pointe Calumet, Quebec
JON 1G1, Canada
514-472-8042

CATAMARAN SAILS

Calvert Sails
250 Industrial Drive
Islamorada, Florida 33036
305-664-8056

Elliot/Pattison Sails
870 Production Place
Newport Beach, CA 92663
714-645-6697

Smyth Team Sails
216 Texas Street
Ft. Walton Beach, Florida 32548
904-243-WIND

CATAMARAN ACCESSORY DEALERS

Murray's Marine
Largest Catamaran Parts
   Dealer in the world.
   Catalog Sales.
P.O. Box 490
Carpinteria, California 93014
805-684-8393

Cheta Outboard Bracket
P.O. Box 1234
Hobe Sound, Florida 33475
407-746-0479
Turns your small cat into a
   motorboat

Cat Trax Beach Dollies
Florida Sailcraft
1601 N.E. 18th Avenue
Ft. Lauderdale, Florida 33305
1-800-292-9777

Mentor Marine Products
(Mesh Trampoline
   Replacement)
P.O. Box 502002
San Diego, CA 92150-2002
1-888-5-Mentor

Harken Cat Hardware
1251 E. Wisconsin Avenue
Pewaukee, WI 53072
414-691-3320

CATAMARAN ASSOCIATIONS

Aqua Cat
American Sail Inc.
Stark Industrial Park
Charkston, South Carolina 29405

Freestyle Cat
1942 E. Pomona
Santa Ana, CA 92705

G-Cat
269 16th Street N.
St. Petersburg, Florida 33713

Hobie Cat
Box 1008
Oceanside, California 92054

Pacific Cat
447 North Newport Blvd.
Newport Beach, California
   92663

Prindle Cat/Nacra Cat
1810 E. Borchard Ave.
Santa Ana, California 92705

Sol Cat
214 East Montecito St.
Santa Barbara, California 93101

Tornado Cat Association U.S.
10319 Rocky Hollow
La Porte, Texas 77571

Windrush Cat
1 Rawlinson Street
O'Connor 6163
Perth, West Australia

SAILING SCHOOLS

Rick White Sailing Seminars
Race-Training Seminars for
   Catamarans
P.O. Box 2060
Key Largo, Florida 33037
305-451-3287

SUGGESTIONS FOR
FURTHER READING

RACING

*Catamaran Racing from Start to
   Finish*, Phil Berman (W. W.
   Norton & Company, New
   York 1988)

Multihull Racing: the Hobie Cats,
   Fred Miller and Phil Berman
   (Aztex Publishing, Inc.
   Arizona 1976)

*Welcome to A-Fleet (Book 1 and
   2)* Jack Sammons (Batjak Publishing, Florida 1976, 78)

Advanced Racing Tactics, Stuart
   Walker (W. W. Norton &
   Company, New York 1976)

Catamaran Racing: For the 90's,
   Rick White (RAM Press, 1992)
   P.O. Box 2060, Key Largo,
   Florida 33037

GENERAL

Fiberglass Repair, Paul Tetricks
   (Cornell Maritime Press, 1970)

Instant Weather Forecasting,
   Alan Watts (Dodd, Mead &
   Company, New York 1978)

PHOTO CREDITS

All photographs in the book are by the author except those listed below.

PHOTOS

Courtesy of Almon Lockabey—169

Courtesy of Budd Symes—59

Courtesy of G-Cat Association—44, 184

Courtesy of Hobie Cat Association (Most by Jake Grubb)—2, 5, 6, 9, 10, 11, 18, 25, 32, 37, 81, 84, 100, 103, 109, 118, 127, 175, 177, 180, 187, 201

Courtesy of Jay Sonnenklar—125

Courtesy of Nacra 5.2 Association—161, 182, 189

Courtesy of Pacific Cat Association—93

Courtesy of Performance Catamaran—7, 12, 13, 14, 15, 20, 119, 121, 123 (both), 126

Courtesy of Prindle Cat Association (most by Leslie Lindeman)—7, 8, 30, 39, 129, 133, 142, 160, 167

Courtesy of Steven Jost—49

Courtesy of Windfast Marine—87

Courtesy of Windrush Yachts—196

ACKNOWLEDGMENTS

Most good things require cooperation, and the people below have proven this to me again. In no specific order, I thank you all.
Bradford Scott, Brad Avery, Steven Vance, Steve Murray, Nancy Colenbaugh, Gretchen Williams, Fran Westerdahl, The College of Creative Studies at the University of California at Santa Barbara, Harry Reese, the people at Daves Camera, Gary McAvoy, and everyone who so kindly posed for my camera.